344.713076
KELS

Charles Sturt University
Library

An Educator's Guide to

FUNDING AND GOVERNANCE

Brian A. Kelsey, Q.C.

D1508653

Aurora Professional Press
a division of Canada Law Book Inc.
240 Edward Street, Aurora, Ontario

© CANADA LAW BOOK INC., 1999
Printed in Canada

All rights reserved. No part of this book may be reproduced in any form by
any photographic, electronic, mechanical or other means, or used in any
information storage and retrieval system, without the written permission of
the publisher.
The paper used in this publication meets the minimum requirements of
American National Standards for Information Sciences — Permanence of
Paper for Printed Library Materials ANSI Z39.48-1992.

Cover Photograph:
Charles Thatcher/Tony Stone Images

Canadian Cataloguing in Publication Data

Kelsey, Brian A., 1934-
  An educator's guide to funding and governance

Includes bibliographical references and index.
ISBN 0-88804-277-9

1. School management and organization – Law and legislation – Ontario.
2. Education – Finance – Law and legislation – Ontario. I. Title.

KE0773.K44 1999   344.713'07   C99-931871-3
KF4125.K 44 1999

This book is dedicated to
the memory of
my mentor and friend,
Bert J. MacKinnon, Q.C.

Foreword

"Upon the education of the people of this country the fate of this country depends." At least so said Benjamin Disraeli. I believe it. The mantle of Elijah may not have been grasped either literally or figuratively but, truly, provision of public education is the greatest of a society's gifts to itself. It is more important than any other factor fostering and determining a democratic society. The funding and governance of education are paramount to its direction and the achievement of its objective.

I suspect that almost everyone has very definite opinions on the subject of schools. Most people have at least been to one and have their own anecdotal experiences. Mine have been formed over a fairly extensive period of time through regular and current contact with the varied aspects of education in my jurisdiction. I have been associated with this enterprise of education since I was first elected as a public school trustee in the east end of Toronto in 1976. I have chaired both the Toronto and the Metropolitan Toronto school boards during the most iconoclastic and fundamental alterations to the funding and governance of education since this province's inception. It was from this vantage point that I had the opportunity of observing Brian Kelsey first-hand as he plied his trade in the legal aspects of those subjects. The fraternity in this area of law is a small one. Based on my observations, the author is the best one of the bunch.

I would agree with Mr. Kelsey that, whatever the final outcome of the matters currently before the courts, the fulcrum in education decision making has been irrevocably shifted in favour of central authority over local. Nevertheless, the topics under discussion remain no less important. An informed debate on the matters at hand would be a welcome relief and the author has provided the essential knowledge basic to that discussion.

This book affords a comprehensive overview of the subject in an insightful and informative fashion — all you need to know on the topic in 187 pages. In many circles, the mere mention of the topic makes the listener's eyes glaze over. The length of this book should not be used as a defence against its being read. If it can be made palatable, Kelsey has done it. He has a way with words, one that is to be envied and emulated. The treatment he affords a complicated, complex and multi-faceted subject is surprisingly simplified, readable and user-friendly. The political decisions, together with the philosophy and pragmatism which are their foundation, are not under consideration. Parochial partnership is set aside. Rather, this is as well-planned map through the current intricacies of the system.

The provision of the historical setting is both interesting and useful. The myriad of today's provincial agencies, commissions, regulations and the inter-connection and overlaying of the various statutes is a maze of biblical propor-tions. The book, however, is organized in a simple, straightforward manner. The author guides us up, down, in, out and around the web and woof of the fabric of education law. He makes it hang together in an understandable and easily referenced format. This is the "Who does what in education" manual.

The book is called an "educator's guide" whereas this is not an educator's foreword. It is that of a layperson who has an abiding faith in the worth of public education. Indeed, the general public ought to have a passionate regard for it rather than a passing one. The children of today through their education are the inheritors of a treasure of knowledge and thought and the heirs of their own exertions. The mundane matters, such as who decides, how and what type of education they will be exposed to and whether or not there will be moneys to pay for it are part and parcel of the loftier goal and one cannot be divorced from the other. Governance, funding, education, society — all are joined at the hip.

There is nothing new about "change" in education. Education is dynamic. It always has been. It always will be. Like a tide, it regularly rolls in and out. The present is the same as the past, only different. Reconciling and understanding this in context is essential for educators and to be devoutly hoped for in the general society.

Toronto, Ontario   David J. Moll
September, 1999

Preface

The structural changes to the education system in Ontario in the past three years have been the most far-ranging since those made in the mid-19th century under the guidance of Egerton Ryerson. The most fundamental changes have been effected in the relationship between the province and the local school boards, in the ways in which revenue is raised and the rules governing the expenditure of that revenue.

Education, like health, raises both vigorous debate and emotional temperatures, but change, once implemented, is seldom reversed. At the time of writing, the constitutional validity of the removal from school boards of their powers to determine their own revenue and expenditure has not been finally determined by the courts. However, whatever may be the outcome, it is unlikely that there will be a return to pre-existing models. It is therefore with some confidence that this book may be put forward as an analysis, not only of how the education system is now funded and governed, but of how in its essentials it will continue in the foreseeable future.

I should at the outset declare my own interest. For the past fifteen years, I have had the rewarding experience of representing public school boards. My views and loyalties have necessarily been influenced, in part formed, by that experience. This does not, of course, affect my analysis of the law which follows but the reader may well detect my firm convictions on the value of local management of school systems and the service which school boards have provided and which, one hopes, they will continue to provide to their communities.

As counsel to the Metropolitan Toronto School Board until its demise on December 31, 1997, I was myself educated in the complexities and politics of the system and became increasingly impressed by the high standards of competence, professionalism and dedication, at both the political and administrative levels. I had the privilege of working with successive directors of the board, Charles Brown, Ned McKeown, Don McVicar and Darrel Skidmore, and with board chairs, John Tolton, Ann Vanstone, Mae Waese and David Moll.

I am also grateful for the opportunity to work with the superintendents of the Metropolitan Toronto School Board, particularly Carole Olsen, through whose good offices I was introduced to education law, Jack Murray, Don Higgins, Brian Lenglet, whose knowledge of the intricacies of funding never ceases to amaze me, and Bill Mitchell, whose sharp eye on legislative issues has always been invaluable. I must also mention the staff in the offices of the chair and director who kept the whole operation on track and who continue to contribute their experience and commitment to education, Rebecca Amyotte, Marlene Riley, Dorothy Dent and Cathy Rechtshaffën.

In the preparation of this book, I have had the benefit of being able to draw on the expertise of a number of people who have provided expert evidence to the courts in the constitutional cases arising out of Bill 104 and Bill 160. Of particular help as sources have been, in funding, the affidavits of Nancy Naylor, as manager of the education finance unit of the Ministry, Brian Lenglet, and in historical background, Professor Robert Gidney, Wyn Millar, Professor Mark G. McGowan and Professor Robert Dixon.

The number of lawyers in education law, especially in the big cases, is relatively small but they are a highly skilled and knowledgeable group. I continue to learn from them all. I am particularly indebted to my co-counsel, Bill Challis (now a senior counsel with the Freedom of Information and Privacy Commission), and Eric Gillespie.

The professionalism and patience of the staff at Aurora Professional Press have been vital in bringing this work to fruition. I am particularly grateful to Howard Davidson for his gentle but firm shepherding of both me and the project, and to Heather Bunner for her keen editorial eye and pen.

Finally, my undying gratitude goes to my wife and administrative assistant, Julie, who typed and retyped the manuscript at bewildering speed, with editorial comments addressed less to its content and more to the organizational shortcomings of its author. For those shortcomings, and for others which this book may reflect, the author is alone responsible.

Toronto, Ontario   Brian A. Kelsey
July, 1999

Table of Contents

1 Constitutional Framework 1

2 The Central Authority 17

6 Organization of Boards 71

7 Members of Boards 77

8 Administration of Boards.......................... 87

9 Former Funding Model 103

10 New Funding Model: Tax Revenue 117

11 New Funding Model: Provincial Grants

12 Capital Funding

13 Finances of Boards

1

Constitutional Framework

WHAT IS GOVERNANCE?

Governance is generally understood to mean the act and manner of governing, or the formal public system for conducting the policy, actions and affairs of a political entity. Inherent in a structure of governance are organs of authority, power and influence.

The democratic governance of education has been described as:

> . . . the result of a complicated interplay among those who exercise authority (the right to make decisions), those who exercise power (the capacity to influence decisions), and those whose lives and interests are affected by this authority and power.[1]

The confining of the exercise of power to the capacity to influence is open to question.

"Authority" is the entitlement or power to perform acts of legal force and effect, the right of power to enforce compliance with the law. The authority to make laws is synonymous with the power to make laws. The preferred dichotomy therefore is between authority and power on the one hand and influence on the other hand. The definitions would accordingly be:

- "Educational governance" is the system established by law for the formal control of the education system through the exercise of authority and influence.
- "Authority" or "power" is the right, conferred by law, to make decisions about a particular matter in the educational system.
- "Influence" is the right, conferred by law, to participate in a particular decision-making process, without having the right to make a final decision.

---

[1] N. Henchey and D.A. Burgess, *Between Past and Future: Quebec Education in Transition* (Calgary, Detselig, 1987), p. 41.

1

In Ontario, the Minister of Education and Training, the legislature and school boards have authority and power. Examples of institutions and individuals with influence but not power are the Ontario Parent Council, the Languages of Instruction Commission of Ontario, pupil representatives on school boards, and school board advisory committees. These may all advise and recommend, and therefore influence, within legally established parameters, but they lack the capacity to exercise power over the actions of others. The Education Improvement Commission, on the other hand, exercises both power and influence. All of the above are part of the system of governance.

THE CONSTITUTION

An examination of education governance begins with the Constitution.[2] The purpose of a constitution is to "establish the scope of governmental authority and to set out the terms of the relationship between the citizen and the state and those between the organs of government".[3]

The Constitution is the ultimate source of all legal authority and the Constitution confers on legislatures the power to pass statutes. Statutes confer powers on the executive, Cabinet and the Ministers and in the education context on school boards and trustees. The legislature also delegates to Cabinet and the Minister the power to make regulations having the force of law and confers upon public agencies powers within defined areas.

Legislation also creates bodies with the ability to advise, recommend or influence. The ability to exercise influence is created by law but its actual exercise is not the exercise of power as it has no direct legal consequences to rights and duties.

A constitution both confers legal authority and limits its exercise. In its most recent analysis of the Canadian Constitution, the Supreme Court of Canada said:

> . . . the Constitution of Canada includes the global system of rules and principles which govern the exercise of constitutional authority in the whole and in every part of the Canadian state . . . a constitution must contain a comprehensive set of rules and principles which are capable of providing an exhaustive legal framework for our system of government.[4]

---

[2] Originally, the *British North America Act, 1867*, but now includes various constitutional statutes enacted between 1867 and 1982, as listed in the Schedule to the *Constitution Act, 1982*.

[3] Swinton, "Application of the Canadian Charter of Rights and Freedoms" in Tarnopolsky and Beaudoin, eds., *Canadian Charter of Rights and Freedoms* (Toronto, Carswell, 1982), p. 44.

[4] *Reference re Secession of Quebec* (1998), 161 D.L.R. (4th) 385 (S.C.C.), at p. 403.

The Court went on to point out that the evolution of our constitutional arrangements has been characterized by adherence to certain underlying constitutional principles:

> . . . federalism, democracy, constitutionalism and the rule of law, and respect for minority rights. These defining principles function in symbiosis. No single principle can be defined in isolation from the others, nor does any one principle trump or exclude the operation of any other.[5]

Each of these principles has application to the governance of education.

Canada is a federal system. In a federal system of government, political power is shared by two levels of government: the federal parliament and government on the one hand; and the provinces on the other. Each is assigned respective spheres of jurisdiction by the Constitution, which defines the respective powers of the federal and provincial legislatures. As will be seen, education, with limited exceptions, is a provincial responsibility.

The basic structure of a constitution in a democracy includes the existence of political institutions, including freely elected legislative bodies at both the federal and provincial levels. The elected legislature expresses the will of the people and makes the laws which govern us. However, the legislature operates within the framework of the constitution and is only one of a number of public institutions exercising authority within the confines of the law. In Canada, these institutions include the Cabinet,[6] agencies of government exercising powers delegated to them by the legislature or the executive, and the judiciary. The role of each of these arms of government in the governance of education will become apparent.

The third principle, constitutionalism, requires that all government action comply with the Constitution. The Constitution governs and binds legislatures and governments, both federal and provincial, and every agency and person whose conduct constitutes action of the state. Their sole claim to exercise lawful authority rests in the powers allocated to them under the Constitution, and from no other source. In the field of education, the Constitution both confers power and imposes limitations upon the exercise of that power.

The principle of the rule of law requires that all state action comply with the law. "The 'rule of law' [has many aspects, but its foundation is] a sense of orderliness, of subjection to known legal rules and of executive accountability to legal authority authority."[7] The rule of law ensures a stable, predictable and ordered society. It provides protection for individuals from arbitrary state ac-

---

[5] *Supra*, at p. 410.

[6] Under the Canadian Constitution, the executive power in a province is the Lieutenant Governor in Council, the Lieutenant Governor acting by and with the advice of the Executive Council, *i.e.*, Cabinet. Throughout this book, the Lieutenant Governor in Council is referred to as Cabinet.

[7] *Reference re Secession of Quebec, supra*, footnote 4, at p. 416-17, quoting *Reference re Resolution to Amend the Constitution* (1981), 125 D.L.R. 1 (S.C.C.), at pp. 875-6.

tion and requires that every action of the state, in education as in every other field, be justified by reference to law.

The fourth underlying constitutional principle concerns the protection of minorities. In Canada, as in many other countries, the Constitution establishes rights and freedoms for individuals and certain groups which may not be infringed or abrogated by government.

In the education context, the Constitution, of which the *Canadian Charter of Rights and Freedoms*[8] forms a part, provides protection for defined denominational and language groups and individuals.

EDUCATION AND THE CONSTITUTION

In order to understand the various forms which education governance has taken in Ontario and the other provinces, it is necessary to understand the constitutional framework specific to education. It is this framework which explains why the school system in each province is differently governed and financed and why the powers of the legislatures to effect change vary from province to province. It is this framework which determines why in Ontario there is a need for four kinds of school boards, why one system of denominational schools is funded to the exclusion of all other denominations and why the public school system is completely secular but Roman Catholic schools can give preference in the hiring and promotion of teachers who are members of their faith.

Constitutional restrictions on the powers of provincial legislatures also explain why the Province of Quebec required legislation by the Canadian Parliament to enable it to transform its system formerly based on denomination into a system based on language, and why the Province of Newfoundland similarly needed a constitutional amendment to enable it to replace its system of denominational schools with a public system.

Some provinces have found the constitutional restrictions a barrier to school reform. Constitutional limitations on the powers of provincial legislatures have been the basis for court challenges in Ontario and Alberta to government moves towards centralization of funding and greater provincial control over the education system. It is not inconceivable that there will be debate in Ontario on the desirability of an expansion of provincial power by constitutional amendment.

---

[8] The *Canadian Charter of Rights and Freedoms*, Part I of the *Constitution Act, 1982*, being Schedule B of the *Canada Act, 1982* (U.K.), 1982, c. 11, was proclaimed in force by the Parliament of Canada on April 17, 1982.

POWER TO MAKE LAWS

The key constitutional provisions governing education are s. 93 of the Constitution and s. 23 of the Charter. The legislative power in Canada with respect to education is vested by s. 93 in the provincial legislatures.

Section 93 explains in part the absence of the federal government in educational policy and governance. The Canadian Parliament has no law-making power with respect to education. However in the United States, although the United States Constitution confers no power on their federal authorities in education, the American federal government has a significant role in education. It may be that, education having been a contentious matter upon which consensus at Confederation was reached with great difficulty, the federal authorities were content that future conflicts be played out solely at the provincial level.

The opening words of s. 93 state:

> **93.** In and for each Province the Legislature may exclusively make Laws in relation to Education, subject and according to the following Provisions:—

However, this "plenary power" may be exercised only "subject and according to" the four subsections which follow, and which deal with the rights of denominational schools. As the Supreme Court of Canada has said, the protection of minority religious rights was a major element during the negotiations leading to Confederation because of the desire of religious minorities in both Upper and Lower Canada for the protection of their schools from the will of the majorities.[9]

> Section 93 is the product of an historical compromise which was a crucial step along the road leading to Confederation. As Gonthier J. said in *Reference re Education Act (Que.)*, [1993] 2 S.C.R. 511 at p. 529, 105 D.L.R. (4th) 266 (S.C.C.):
>
> > "Section 93 is unanimously recognized as the expression of a desire for political compromise. It served to moderate religious conflicts which threatened the birth of the Union."
>
> Without this "solemn pact", this "cardinal term" of Union, there would have been no Confederation.[10]

A close reading of s. 93 reveals the elements of which it is composed. First, it distributes power and rights among a number of groups and institutions:

---

[9] See *Reference re An Act to Amend the Education Act (Ontario)* (1987), 40 D.L.R. (4th) 18 (S.C.C.), *per* Wilson J., at pp. 42-4 [the *Bill 30 Reference*]. See also *Education Amendment Act*, S.O. 1986, c. 21 (Bill 30).

[10] *Adler v. Ontario* (1996), 140 D.L.R. (4th) 385 (S.C.C.), *per* Iacobucci J., at p. 401 [the *Private School Funding Case*].

1. The legislative power is exclusively vested in the provinces.
2. The federal Cabinet is empowered to intervene in specific, limited circumstances in relation to denominational schools. Cabinet may consider an appeal from any Act or decision of any provincial authority affecting any right or privilege of the Protestant or Roman Catholic minorities in relation to education, where in that province a system of separate or dissentient schools existed by law at the union or is thereafter established by the legislature of the province.
3. The Parliament of Canada is given the power to make remedial laws for the due execution of the provisions of s. 93 and of any decision of the Cabinet on an appeal.

Although not specifically mentioned in s. 93, the courts also have a role in its interpretation, primarily in defining the scope of the denominational protections.

Secondly, s. 93 establishes certain protections for denominational schools against legislative interference. A class of persons which had rights and privileges at Confederation with respect to denominational schools is entitled to the continued enjoyment of these rights and privileges free from legislative abridgement. The trustees of Roman Catholic and Protestant school boards in Quebec have enjoyed constitutional protection, not only for the powers and privileges which they had under the laws of Lower Canada, but also for the powers and privileges which Roman Catholic trustees had in 1867 in Upper Canada.

The purpose of the second of these provisions was explained by Lord Carnarvon in his address to the British Parliament proposing second reading of the *British North America Act, 1867*:

> . . . the object of the clause [s. 93] is to secure to the religious minority of one province the same rights, privileges and protection which the religious minority of another Province may enjoy. The Roman Catholic minority of Upper Canada, the Protestant minority of Lower Canada and the Roman Catholic minority of the Maritime Provinces, will thus stand on a footing of entire equality.[11]

Thirdly, s. 93 makes clear the distinction between the denominational schools in Ontario and those in Quebec. The protected denominational schools in Ontario are separate schools. In Quebec, the protected schools are dissentient schools, Roman Catholic and Protestant.

---

[11] Quoted in the *Bill 30 Reference, supra*, footnote 9, at p. 42.

CONSTITUTIONAL PROTECTIONS

The first of the four subsections of s. 93 is the most important. Its deceptively simple wording has been, and continues to be, the subject of extensive litigation. It states:

> (1) Nothing in any such Law shall prejudicially affect any Right or Privilege with respect to Denominational Schools which any Class of Persons have by Law in the Province at the Union:

This subsection crystallizes the rights and privileges relating to denominational schools under the law in effect at the time each province entered Confederation. It has been termed "in a sense a snapshot of the legislative situation in 1867".[12]

The purpose of s. 93(1) was to provide protection for Roman Catholic education in the Province of Ontario, and in the Province of Quebec for Protestant (and Roman Catholics where they were in local minority) education. The section applied originally to the first four provinces. The substance of the section, with modifications, was applied to the other provinces as they each joined Confederation.

In order to claim the protection of the section, the following conditions must be meet. There must be

    (a) a right or privilege affecting a denominational school,
    (b) enjoyed by a particular class of persons,
    (c) by law,
    (d) in effect at the time of Confederation, and
    (e) which is prejudicially affected by provincial legislation.

The law relating to denominational schools varied in each province at the time of its entry into Confederation. Accordingly, the scope of the rights and privileges protected under the section is determined by ascertaining the rights and privileges in existence in each province at the time of union.

Ontario

The only "class of persons" which in Ontario in 1867 had a legal right to denominational schools was that of Roman Catholics. The relevant law in existence in 1867 was the *Act to restore to Roman Catholics in Upper Canada certain rights in respect to Separate Schools*,[13] which in effect gave Roman

---

[12] *Reference re Education Act (Que.)* (1993), 105 D.L.R. (4th) 266 (S.C.C.), at p. 284.
[13] S.U.C. 1863 (2nd Sess.), c. 5 [the *Scott Act*].

Catholics the right to an independent administration of their schools. Unlike in Quebec, schools for Roman Catholics in Ontario were not "dissentient schools". Roman Catholics in Ontario did not have to be in the minority or in disagreement with the regulations of the public system in order to establish a school of their denomination. It was sufficient that there be at least five Roman Catholics wishing to create their own school.

The *Scott Act* conferred on the trustees of separate schools the power to impose, levy and collect school rates from persons sending their children to or subscribing towards the support of such schools, and all the powers in respect of separate schools that the trustees of common schools had under the provisions of the Act relating to common schools. In addition, every separate school was entitled to a share in the fund annually granted by the legislature for the support of common schools, and in all other public grants, investments and allotments for common school purposes, according to the average number of pupils attending the school.

Roman Catholic parents could choose to support either the local separate schools or the local common schools. If they chose to support with their property taxes the denominational schools, they became separate school supporters, exempt from the payment of taxes to the public system.

Until 1984 this choice was exercised with respect to the elementary school system only, as Roman Catholic separate schools received public funding for elementary education only. In that year, by Bill 30, the province extended to Roman Catholics the right to support their secondary schools with their local taxes and extended full provincial funding to Roman Catholic secondary schools.

The extension of these rights to one denomination only was challenged on the basis of Charter provisions for equality of treatment and freedom of religion. The Supreme Court of Canada rejected the constitutional challenge. Roman Catholic separate school supporters were held to have had at Confederation a right or privilege by law to have their children receive an education at the secondary school level and this right or privilege was constitutionally guaranteed under s. 93(1). The Charter, the Court said, "cannot be applied so as to abrogate or derogate from rights or privileges guaranteed by or under [other provisions of] the Constitution".[14] In case it be thought that s. 93 is a historical relic, it should be realized that in 1982 s. 93 rights were expressly preserved by the Charter. Section 29 of the Charter states:

> **29.** Nothing in this Charter abrogates or derogates from any rights or privileges guaranteed by or under the Constitution of Canada in respect of denominational, separate or dissentient schools.

---

[14] *Bill 30 Reference, supra,* footnote 9, at p. 59.

Section 29, although not strictly necessary to preserve s. 93 rights,

> . . . was put there simply to emphasize that the special treatment guaranteed by the Constitution to denominational, separate or dissentient schools, even if it sits uncomfortably with the concept of equality embodied in the Charter because not available to other schools, is nevertheless not impaired by the Charter.[15]

Quebec

The Act in effect in Lower Canada in 1867[16] provided for two kinds of systems. The general system applied to "rural areas", that is, throughout Lower Canada apart from the cities of Quebec and Montreal. For the municipalities of Quebec and Montreal, the 1861 Act created two independent school networks, one under the control of Roman Catholic commissioners and the other under that of Protestant commissioners. The administration and control conferred by the 1861 Act on the members of a particular denomination gave a denominational character, Catholic or Protestant, to the school systems in these two municipalities *de jure*.

In the rural areas of Quebec, religious minorities alone were entitled to denominational schools, by means of dissenting rights. Section 93 of the Constitution guaranteed "rural" inhabitants of Quebec a right to dissent. This right did not necessarily include the form of the institutions which made it possible to exercise that right since 1867. While the right to dissent obviously includes a means and framework for its exercise, those existing in 1867 are not in themselves constitutionally guaranteed. Accordingly, the Supreme Court of Canada has held that in Quebec the protection afforded to dissentient schools is that which is necessary to protect the "denominational aspects" of the dissenting school system.

In a series of cases from 1984 onwards, the Supreme Court of Canada was called upon to define the limits of the legislative power on the one hand and denominational protection on the other. Although the rights of the dissentient schools were significantly diminished, the denominational boards in the cities of Montreal and Quebec remained inviolate.

The province, frustrated in its attempt to establish a system throughout Quebec based on language, sought and obtained in 1997 a constitutional amendment making s. 93(1) of no application in that province. School boards are now established on a linguistic basis, but Catholic and Protestant committees remain to ensure the continuing influence of religious education.

In April, 1999, a government task force recommended that the province establish a secular system of public schools, with provision for the study of religions from a cultural perspective. Denominational instruction would be

---

[15] *Supra*, at p. 60, *per* Wilson J.

[16] *Act respecting Provincial Aid for Superior Education — and Normal and Common Schools*, C.S.L.C. 1861, c. 15.

restricted to after the school day by any religious group. The preferred position enjoyed by Protestants and Catholics alone would disappear.[17]

The Maritime Provinces

Section 93 of the *Constitution Act, 1867* applies to Nova Scotia and to New Brunswick and was applied to Prince Edward Island when it joined Confederation in 1873. In each province, denominational schools existed but were not recognized "by law" and there was no legal right to public funding.

In Nova Scotia, the school system was and remains non-sectarian. Catholic and Protestant students attend the same schools. In the first half of this century, there were Catholic schools run by the church. These schools were incorporated into the secular public system in the 1950s. Some schools within the public system are permitted by tacit agreement to operate as Catholic schools.

In New Brunswick in 1867, Methodist, Anglican, Roman Catholic and Baptist schools received public funding but there was no tax-supported right in law. In some areas, there are "Roman Catholic" and "Protestant" schools within the publicly supported school system.

In Prince Edward Island, denominational schools existed and received full public support as a result of tacit agreements. In the first half of this century, the schools were "de facto" denominational. Catholics and Protestants generally favoured and chose to attend different schools in the same geographical district. Today, the public school system is secular; students of all religions attend the same schools. The provincial legislation provides that all schools are to be non-sectarian.

Newfoundland

The constitutional guarantee in s. 17 of the *Terms of Union of Newfoundland with Canada*[18] guarantees rights and privileges recognized "by law" of denominational schools and colleges. At the date of union, the law recognized the schools of the Anglican Church, the United Church, Salvation Army denominations collectively referred to as "The Integrated Districts", the Roman Catholic Church, the Seventh Day Adventists and the Presbyterian Church. In 1969, the Anglican Church, the United Church and the Salvation Army combined their separate school systems to form one integrated system. In the same year, by amendment to the Constitution, the Pentecostal Assemblies of Newfoundland were to be added as a denomination under s. 17.

---

[17] The preferred position is maintained, despite the repeal of s. 93(1) in Quebec, by use of the "notwithstanding" clause. The task force report is not necessarily the end of the affair: see C. Hébert, "Quebec's Unholy Battle Between Church and State: Call to Take Religion Out of Public Schools Sparks Furious Debate", *The Toronto Star* (April 16, 1999).

[18] *Newfoundland Act, 1949*, Sch.

In 1997, the government sought and obtained an amendment to the Constitution to provide for a public school system and to take away the control of churches from the publicly funded schools. As a result of that amendment, the Newfoundland legislature now has exclusive authority to make laws in relation to education, subject only to an obligation to provide for courses in religion that are not specific to a religious denomination, and to permit religious observances in a school where requested by parents.

The Western Provinces

The *Constitution Act, 1867* generally applies to Manitoba as though Manitoba had been one of the original four provinces. The language of s. 93(1) was expanded to protect rights or privileges held by law or practice at the date of Manitoba's union with the other provinces.

In 1870 all Manitoba schools were denominational and were regulated and controlled by either the Roman Catholic Church or the various Protestant denominations. The *Public Schools Act*[19] of 1890 ended public funding for separate schools and compelled all ratepayers to support the public school system. This resulted in what became known as the "Manitoba School Question".

Manitoba is the only province in which an appeal has been taken to Cabinet. The Privy Council held that the right of appeal extended to rights and privileges granted after Confederation as well as to those existing at Confederation. However, the Privy Council also held that denominational rights extended only to the right to establish and maintain separate schools, not to public tax revenues or a release from the obligation to pay taxes towards public schools.

The Manitoba School Question was resolved politically in 1896 by an agreement between Ottawa and Manitoba which provided for some religious instruction in public schools and for petitions by Roman Catholics that the school trustees employ a Roman Catholic teacher.

When Alberta and Saskatchewan became provinces in 1905, s. 93(1) was replaced by a slightly different provision protecting the rights or privileges which separate schools had at union under the terms of cc. 29 and 30 of the Ordinances of the Northwest Territories passed in 1901, and rights or privileges with respect to religious instruction in public and separate schools as provided for in those Ordinances. Separate schools in both provinces became constitutionally entitled to the same rights, powers and privileges which public schools had by law.

Section 93 applies to British Columbia as though it was one of the original provinces but there were no rights or privileges with respect to denominational schools in British Columbia at its union. British Columbia funds denomina-

---

[19] S.M. 1890, c. 38.

tional schools as private schools; Roman Catholic schools comprise the largest group of denominational schools.

GOVERNANCE OF MINORITY LANGUAGE EDUCATION

Denominational rights vary from province to province. Minority language rights do not. They are uniform across Canada. All citizens of Canada in a linguistic minority have exactly the same rights with respect to education in each province. The expression of these rights varies according to the particular circumstances but, in the context of local conditions, not on a province-by-province basis.

Rights of governance based on language were created in 1982 by s. 23 of the *Canadian Charter of Rights and Freedoms*. As a result of s. 23, there are three groups of citizens of Canada in Ontario who have the right to have their children receive primary and secondary instruction in the language of the French linguistic minority:

(i)   those whose first language learned and still understood is French;

(ii) those who have received their primary school instruction in Canada in French and reside in Ontario; and

(iii) those with any child who has received or is receiving primary or secondary school instruction in French in Canada.

The right to receive from public funds "minority language instruction" means, in a historical and political context, the right to become sufficiently fluent in that language to participate fully in one or the other of the two language communities in Canada protected by s. 23. The section mandates effective language instruction.

Section 23 affords to the minority language group the right, where numbers warrant, to establish and control an independent school system. The province selects the institutional means by which that right will be implemented.

In some circumstances, francophones may be entitled to the same form of governance as the majority, that is, an independent francophone school board. However where the number of students enrolled in minority schools is relatively small, other solutions may satisfy the mandate of s. 23.

To satisfy s. 23, it is essential that the minority language group have control over those aspects of education which relate to its language and culture. This degree of control may be achieved by guaranteeing representation of the minority on a shared school board and by giving these representatives exclusive control over all of the aspects of minority education which have linguistic and cultural concerns.

The right to tax (which usually accompanies the creation of an independent school district), is not essential to achieve linguistic and cultural security. Section 23 guarantees that minority schools shall receive public funds but it is not necessary that the funds be derived through a separate tax base, provided adequate funding is otherwise assured.

The "where numbers warrant" provision requires, in general, that the educational services appropriate for the numbers of students involved and the cost of those services be taken into account in determining what s. 23 requires.

A threshold number of students is required before certain programs or facilities can operate effectively and s. 23 recognizes that it may be financially impractical to accord to every group of minority language students, no matter how small, the same services which a large group is accorded.[20]

Section 23 is unusual and provides a different type of legal right. While s. 93 preserves a system of governance already in existence, s. 23 confers upon a group a right by placing obligations on government to alter or develop major institutional structures to create a system of governance which satisfies constitutional demands. As will be seen, the Province of Ontario has created a network of French-language boards, both public and Roman Catholic, throughout the province.

CONSTITUTIONAL POSITION OF PUBLIC SCHOOLS

The conventional view has always been that constitutional protection in governance has existed only for specific denominational school systems and, more recently, for linguistic minorities. Until recently, all the court challenges had been under s. 93(1) to legislation extending or restricting denominational school rights, and then to provincial failures to meet the mandate of s. 23. In the denominational context, the court challenges have been:

(a) by separate (or, in Quebec, denominational or dissentient) school interests to legislation alleged to be an infringement or impairment of their constitutional rights; and

(b) by public board interests to legislative expansion of separate school rights.

All these cases involved the extent of the explicit constitutional rights of separate or denominational schools and established that:

---

[20] The nature and extent of s. 23 has been defined by the courts in: *Reference re Education Act of Ontario and Minority Language Education Rights* (1984), 10 D.L.R. (4th) 491 (Ont. C.A.); *Mahe v. Alberta* (1990), 68 D.L.R. (4th) 69 (S.C.C.); *Reference re Public Schools Act (Man.) s. 79(3), (4) and (7)* (1993), 100 D.L.R. (4th) 723 (S.C.C.).

1. The provincial legislature may supplement but not diminish the constitutional rights and privileges of separate schools.
2. It is not open to public school interests to challenge legislation which augments the rights and privileges of separate schools and separate school supporters.
3. Only denominational school interests are entitled to the aid of the courts to determine the scope of the protected rights of denominational schools.

Judges have been accustomed to considering s. 93 solely in the context of the explicit rights granted, in particular by s. 93(1) and to a limited extent by s. 93(2). As one judge put it, "The intention [of s. 93 (1)] was to protect the minority, leaving the majority to protect themselves through the use of the democratic instrument, the ballot box."[21] However, recent radical change in education funding and governance in some provinces, affecting both separate schools and public schools, has provoked court challenges on behalf of public school supporters and boards.

It is argued that these cases require that s. 93 be read and interpreted from a new perspective. For the first time in Ontario and elsewhere, legislatures have moved to diminish the powers and status of both separate and public school boards, a development not within the contemplation of the Fathers of Confederation or their successors. Separate schools having moved over a period of 150 years within striking distance of achieving an autonomy in parity with public schools, the issue now before the courts is whether the legislature may substantially diminish the autonomy of the system of local school board governance and funding, both public and separate.

To date, the public school arguments have not been successful. Decisions of the Alberta Court of Appeal and two judges in Ontario have denied any constitutional protection of public schools by way of "mirror equality" with separate schools.[22]

However, a majority of the justices of the Supreme Court of Canada, in a case asserting constitutional rights for independent denominational schools,

---

[21] *Calgary Board of Education v. Alberta (Attorney General)* (1981), 122 D.L.R. (3d) 249 (Alta. C.A.), leave to appeal to S.C.C. refused 122 D.L.R. (3d) 249*fn, per* McDermid J.A., at p. 251. For a concise summary of the general principles of s. 23, see *British Columbia (Association des Parents Francophones) v. British Columbia* (1996), 139 D.L.R. (4th) 356 (B.C.S.C.), *per* Vickers J., at pp. 370-72.

[22] *Public School Boards' Assn. of Alberta v. Alberta (Attorney General)* (1998), 158 D.L.R. (4th) 267 (Alta. C.A.); *Ontario Public School Boards' Assn. v. Ontario (Attorney General)* (1997), 151 D.L.R. (4th) 346 (Ont. Ct. (Gen. Div.)) [the *Bill 104 Case*]; *Ontario English Catholic Teachers' Assn. v. Ontario (Attorney General)* (1998), 162 D.L.R. (4th) 257 (Ont. Ct. (Gen. Div.)), appeal allowed in part 172 D.L.R. (4th) 193 (C.A.) [the *Bill 160 Case*]. The latter two cases are court challenges to Bill 104, *Fewer School Boards Act, 1997,* S.O. 1997, c. 3, and Bill 160, *Educational Quality Improvement Act, 1997,* S.O. 1997, c. 31.

broke new ground with respect to the position of public schools in s. 93. The justice writing the majority judgement said:

> In my view, [the Appellants'] argument is mistaken in supposing that public schools are not contemplated by the terms of s. 93 as it applied to Ontario. On the contrary, the public school system is an integral part of the s. 93 scheme. When the province funds public schools, it is, in the words of Wilson J. in *Reference re Bill 30*, at p. 1198, legislating "pursuant to the plenary power in relation to education granted to the provincial legislatures as part of the Confederation compromise". A closer examination of s. 93, in particular s. 93 (1), as it applies to the Province of Ontario, will help to illustrate that the public school system is impliedly, but nonetheless clearly, contemplated by the terms of that section.[23]

The rights of the public system were not directly in issue in that case and it remains to be seen how far the Court is prepared, when the Alberta and Ontario cases reach the Supreme Court, to extend these statements to afford constitutional status to public schools equivalent to that of separate schools.[24]

INDEPENDENT SCHOOLS

These schools receive no direct financial benefit or aid from the Province of Ontario. Following the introduction into the Constitution of the *Canadian Charter of Rights and Freedoms* in 1982, representatives of Jewish day schools and Protestant Christian schools challenged the failure of the province to fund them on the grounds of alleged violations of s. 2(*a*) (freedom of conscience and religion) and s. 15(1) (equality rights) of the Charter.

The applicants failed on both grounds. Section 93 was held by a majority of the justices in the Supreme Court of Canada to be a complete code of denominational school rights.[25] The only constitutional obligation of the province was in relation to Roman Catholic schools under s. 93(1) of the Constitution. Subject to s. 93 (1), the province remains free to exercise its plenary power with regard to education in whatever way it sees fit. The province may, if it so decides, pass legislation extending funding to denominational schools other than Roman Catholic schools without infringing the rights guaranteed to Roman Catholic separate schools under s. 93(1). However, an ability to pass such legislation does not amount to an obligation to do so and the Province of Ontario, unlike the western provinces, has not done so.

---

[23] *Private School Funding Case* (1996), 140 D.L.R. (4th) 385 (S.C.C.), at p. 404.

[24] In the *Bill 160 Case*, *supra*, footnote 22, the Ontario Court of Appeal held that separate school boards have no constitutionally protected rights of fiscal autonomy, but only to funding sufficient to provide a suitable education. It was therefore unnecessary to consider the position of public schools.

[25] *Private School Funding Case*, *supra*, footnote 23.

2

The Central Authority

PARTNERSHIP

The early legislation on education in Upper Canada[1] established at the outset the principle of a sharing of authority, power and influence between the central authority and local government and that principle continues to form the basis of the system of governance today.

The seeds were sown early for what has been described as "the tension between centralized, bureaucratic authority and local, community-based control".[2] Education was administered not only by "local government", but also by organs of government for the running of schools which were quite separate and distinct from other municipal institutions.

Local councils had a limited role in education. County councils had to raise by assessment a sum of money to be applied to teachers' salaries at least equal to the legislative grant apportioned to the townships of the county. Urban municipal councils and township councils were required to levy rates for school purposes on property in school sections as requested by school trustees. This was the extent of their participation in education.

The decisions on buying a school site, building or renting a schoolhouse, purchasing textbooks and apparatus, hiring teachers and augmenting a teacher's salary were made by boards of school trustees. There was no Minister or Ministry of Education in pre-Confederation Ontario. The central authority consisted of a tripartite structure, the Council of Public Instruction, the Chief Superintendent and the Education Office or Education Department.

The members of the Council of Public Instruction were appointed by the Governor. The principal duties of the council were:

---

[1] *Act to establish Public Schools in each and every District of this Province*, S.U.C.. 1807, c. 6; *Common Schools Act*, S.U.C. 1816, c. 36.

[2] P. Axelrod, *The Promise of Schooling: Education in Canada 1800-1914* (Toronto, University of Toronto Press, 1997), pp. 36-7.

(a) to regulate teacher training;

(b) to make regulations for the organization, government and discipline of the schools;

(c) to make regulations for the classification of schools and teachers; and

(d) to recommend or disapprove of school textbooks.[3]

The duties of the Chief Superintendent were:

(a) to apportion the legislative school grant to the common and grammar schools according to law so that all moneys were applied to the objects for which they were granted;

(b) to encourage the use of approved textbooks;

(c) to bring before the Council of Public Instruction regulations for the organization and government of common schools;

(d) to make an annual financial report to the legislature; and

(e) to oversee the organization and management of the education system generally and account for its progress to the legislature and the Governor.[4]

The Department of Education was the Chief Superintendent's administrative arm. It administered the system according to the law and regulations on education under the supervision of the Chief Superintendent. Even by Confederation, the Department of Education was not mentioned in the legislation and consisted of fewer than ten people. However, it administered a "province-wide school system of hundreds of thousands of students, over five thousand teachers, fifteen thousand school trustees, hundreds of township school superintendents, members of county, town, city, village and township councils".[5]

Egerton Ryerson, Chief Superintendent from 1844 to 1876 and the chief architect of the province's educational system, was firmly committed to the building of a strong school system by both the central and local authorities. The legal powers of the central authority enabled it to establish minimum educational standards and ensure fiscal responsibility. However, the coercive power of the state rested primarily in the power to withhold the government grant when the law was not obeyed. This was the most modest of sanctions as the legislative grant constituted a small percentage of the total spending on education. Most was raised at the local level. The central authority was obliged to rely on advice, persuasion and exhortation.

---

[3] *Common Schools Act,* S.U.C. 1850, c. 48, Part X.

[4] *Ibid.,* Part IX.

[5] B. Curtis, *Building the Educational State: Canada West, 1836 -1871* (London, Ont., Althouse Press, 1988), pp. 131-2.

Exercising his considerable personal authority, Ryerson had to persuade Upper Canadians of the vital importance of public education, of the need to invest in it, of the value of hiring the best teachers and building good schools, and of following sound models of teaching practice. Ryerson's role as Chief Superintendent has been described as "the public instructor" of teachers and trustees. He spent much of his energy in informing and advising local authorities, explaining their responsibilities and arbitrating local disputes. His authority depended ultimately on powers of persuasion and leadership rather than the directives and sanctions of bureaucratic regulation.

The relationship of the Education Office or Education Department was with ratepayers and their elected trustees rather than directly with teachers and pupils. A large degree of independence enabled trustees to challenge and shape central policy in significant ways and play a positive role in creating the system that was formed before Confederation.

The functions of the Council of Public Instruction, the Chief Superintendent and the Education Office were over time consolidated in the Department of Education, then the Ministry of Education and more recently the Ministry of Education and Training.

The "directives and sanctions of bureaucratic regulation" have replaced advice and persuasion and many of the functions of local authorities have been taken over by the province which has taken a greater direct interest in the operation of schools, their staff and pupils. Advice to the government is largely provided by agencies which it itself has created, defined and staffed.

Today, the central authority consists of:

(i) the legislature, which makes decisions from time to time on the appropriate distribution of power and authority between the provincial executive and local authorities;

(ii) the Ministry of Education and Training and the Minister who by authority conferred by the legislature exercise powers by making regulations, issuing administrative directives and delegating powers to subordinate agencies; and

(iii) subordinate agencies created by statute and exercising the specified and specialized powers conferred upon them.

MINISTRY OF EDUCATION AND TRAINING

The role of the Minister of Education and Training is stated concisely in s. 2 of the *Education Act*:

2(2) **Minister to have charge.**— The Minister shall preside over and have charge of the Ministry.

(3) **Administration.**— The Minister is responsible for the administration of this Act and the regulations and of such other Acts and the regulations thereunder as may be assigned to the Minister by the Lieutenant Governor in Council.[6]

The Minister determines and controls the general direction of elementary and secondary education in the province by formulating policy which is implemented by directives, by regulations and by delegation of powers to other provincial agencies.[7] For the most part, the Act confers on the Minister powers, not duties.

One area in which the Act imposes obligations on the Minister is special education.[8] However, by regulation, these responsibilities have been delegated to school boards.[9] This does not, of course, relieve the Minister from the obligations imposed by the Act.

ADMINISTRATIVE DIRECTIVES

The educational aspects of the system are governed by administrative directives from the Ministry, consisting of policy circulars, memoranda, guidelines and bulletins. These administrative functions include powers with respect to:

- the naming of diplomas and certificates
- prescribing courses and areas of study
- selecting and approving textbooks and reference books, and publishing book lists
- granting and withdrawing letters of permission and temporary letters of approval for teachers
- suspending and cancelling certificates of qualification and letters of standing
- determining equivalent qualifications
- prescribing courses of study for teachers, principals, supervisory officers and counselors, and correspondence courses
- providing for scholarships, bursaries and awards
- governing teachers' colleges
- establishing terms for provincial schools

---

[6] R.S.O. 1990, E.2 (as amended to 1998, c. 33).

[7] Although the Minister and the Ministry are at the apex of the power pyramid, they are the instruments of power least written about. It is expected that their role will become clear in this book through the many references to what they do.

[8] *Education Act*, s. 8(3).

[9] *Special Education Programs and Services*, R.R.O. 1990, Reg. 306; *Special Education Advisory Committees*, O. Reg. 464/97; *Identification and Placement of Exceptional Pupils*, O. Reg. 181/98. See discussion in Chapter 5, "Duties and Powers of School Boards".

- making agreements for learning materials and copyright licences
- apportioning federal grants
- supporting educational advancement programs, activities and projects for accountable advances
- supporting educational research and making grants for promotion for advancement of education
- permitting boards to establish French-language programs for English-speaking pupils
- issuing guidelines on school closings
- prescribing duties of auditors
- paying for education costs outside Ontario
- requiring boards to develop ethnocultural equity and anti-racism policies
- establishing a drug education policy framework and requiring boards to develop and implement drug education policies in accordance with the framework
- establishing schools for the deaf and schools for the blind
- establishing demonstration schools for exceptional pupils
- establishing camps for leadership training[10]

Additional administrative powers were granted under Bill 104 and Bill 160, which reflect particular aspects of the government's reform program. They include:

(a) assessing academic achievement and establishing policies and guidelines to do so;

(b) establishing guidelines for the role and responsibilities of board members and officials;

(c) establishing polices and guidelines for pupil representatives on boards; and

(d) directing boards to prepare reports to the Minister on any matter which the Minister requires.[11]

REGULATIONS

With Cabinet approval, the Minister has the power to make regulations with respect to schools and classes established under the Act and schools supported by public money.[12] In addition to the general power to regulate the estab-

---

[10] *Education Act*, s. 8(1).
[11] *Education Act*, s. 8(1), (3.3-3.6), (17.1), (27.1), (27.2).
[12] Section 11(1).

lishment, organization, administration and government of the system, the Minister has the specific power to make regulations with respect to:

- the admission of pupils, pupil records and their disposition
- special education programs and identification and placement appeals
- evening classes and recreation programs
- the purchase of books, accommodation and equipment
- the form of teachers' contracts, certificates and letters of standing, qualification record cards, letters of permission and qualifications to teach, and exchange teachers
- continuing education courses and classes
- supervisory officers, examinations and fees
- religious exercises and education
- language of instruction and sign language
- school libraries and textbooks
- powers and duties of teachers and pupils
- the transportation of pupils
- the practice and procedure at hearings
- duties of directors of education and other supervisory officers
- practices and procedures for suspension or dismissal of a director of education or other supervisory officer
- heritage language programs
- the school year, terms, holidays, calendar and instructional days
- excusing children over 14 from school attendance
- regulating schools for the deaf, schools for the blind and demonstration schools for exceptional pupils[13]

Bill 104 and Bill 160 effected a considerable extension of the powers of the Minister to govern by regulation and the enactment of these Bills was followed by a rapid increase in the number and scope of the regulations. In 1990 there were 31 education regulations in operation. Leaving aside the annual regulations adjusting numbers of dollars, in the six years 1991 to 1996, there were 7 new regulations made and 46 regulations amending existing regulations. In the two years following the passage of Bill 104, 1997 and 1998, there were 54 new regulations made and 49 amending regulations. In other words, in those two years there were almost 8 times the number of new regulations made as were made in the preceding 6 years.

---

[13] *Education Act*, s. 11.

BILL 104

There is no doubt that a parliament or legislature may delegate to the executive the power to make regulations which have the force of law. As early as 1918, the Supreme Court of Canada said:

> The practice of authorizing administrative bodies to make regulations to carry out the object of an Act, instead of setting out all the details in the Act itself, is well known and its legality unquestioned.
>
> . . . . .
>
> Parliament cannot, indeed, abdicate its functions, but within reasonable limits at any rate it can delegate its powers to the executive government. Such powers must necessarily be subject to determination at any time by parliament, and needless to say the acts of the executive, under its delegated authority, must fall within the ambit of the legislative pronouncement by which its authority is measured.[14]

Bill 104 conferred extensive powers on Cabinet to make regulations to implement the restructuring provided for by the Bill. Some of these powers were unexceptional. The regulations could provide for the establishment of new district school boards, their names and areas of jurisdiction, and representation on and elections to those boards.

However, regulations could also be made on "such transitional matters as the Lieutenant Governor in Council considers necessary or advisable in connection with the establishment of district school boards".[15]

Bill 104 also contained what the judge who reviewed the Bill described as "the breathtakingly arbitrary power to make government regulations [including retroactive regulations] which contravene the very statute under which the regulations are made".[16] This last-named power was contained in the *Education Act* in the words:

> . . . in the event of a conflict between a regulation made under this Part and a provision of this Act or of any other Act or regulation, the regulation made under this Part prevails.[17]

This power, to amend by regulation the statute which authorizes the regulation, is known as a "King Henry VIII clause", named after the monarch who gave himself the power to legislate by proclamation.[18]

---

[14] *Re Gray* (1918), 42 D.L.R. 1 (S.C.C.), *per* Fitzpatrick C.J., at pp. 2-3.

[15] Section 327(3)(h) (repealed by Bill 160).

[16] *Bill 104 Case* (1997), 151 D.L.R. (4th) 346 (Ont. Ct. (Gen. Div.)), at p. 357.

[17] Section 349(2) (enacted 1997, c. 3, s. 10; repealed by Bill 160).

[18] "A clause, so named in disrespectful commemoration of Henry VIII's tendency to absolutism, occasionally found in legislation conferring delegated legislative power, giving the delegate power to amend the delegating Act or, usually, any other Act, in order to bring the enabling Act into full operation, or otherwise by Order to remove any difficulty. It seems to date from the *Local Government Act, 1888*, but was in-

In the court challenge to the conferring of this "breathtaking power", Campbell J. pointed out that it is the opposite of the general rule that a statute always prevails, and that such a power:

> . . . is constitutionally suspect because it confers upon the government the unprotected authority to pull itself up by its own legal bootstraps and override arbitrarily, with no further advice from the Legislative Assembly, and no right to be heard by those who may be adversely affected by the change, the very legislative instrument from which the government derives its original authority.[19]

However, relying mainly on the decision of the Supreme Court of Canada upholding the delegation of such a power to the Dominion government in the emergency conditions of the First World War,[20] the judge upheld the validity of the power. The judge said that, as the power had not yet been used, it remained to be seen whether these arbitrary powers were actually necessary to achieve any valid legislative purpose and, "Until there is an actual attempt to use these remarkable powers it is premature to adjudicate upon them in the absence of any concrete facts or actual violation of anyone's rights."[21]

Two points need to be made. First, this approach is inconsistent with a decision of the Privy Council holding that a power conferred by legislation would undoubtedly "be exercised with wisdom and moderation, but it is the creation of the power [to interfere with a constitutional right] and not its exercise that is subject to objection, and the objection would not be removed even though the powers conferred were never exercised at all".[22]

Secondly, if the power itself is valid, it is difficult to envision circumstances in which its actual exercise could be challenged. Such a challenge would have to be founded on a violation of some other right, not merely upon the scope of the power itself, which on its face is unlimited and already held to be valid.

In any event, the power was not exercised and it, together with most of the other delegated powers which had been challenged before Campbell J., disappeared upon the enactment of Bill 160.

---

cluded in some later Acts. The Committee on Ministers' Powers recommended the abandonment of the practice save for the purpose of bringing the Act into operation but instances of its use continue." (D.M. Walker, *The Oxford Companion to Law* (Oxford, Clarendon Press, 1980)).

[19] *Bill 104 Case, supra,* footnote 16, at p. 363.
[20] *Re Gray, supra,* footnote 14.
[21] *Bill 104 Case, supra,* footnote 16, at p. 365.
[22] *Ottawa Separate School Trustees* v. *Ottawa* (1916), 32 D.L.R. 10 (P.C.), at p. 13.

BILL 160

Bill 160, however, added to the Act a number of other sections which conferred new and additional powers on the executive to govern by regulation. These include regulations dealing with the following matters:

- extending the definition of permanent improvements (s. 1(6))
- defining supporter non-resident attendance rights (s. 43.1)
- defining non-supporter resident attendance rights based on business property (s. 46.1(4))
- representation of pupils on school boards (s. 55)
- territory without municipal organization in area of jurisdiction of a school authority (s. 56)
- governing special education tribunals and advisory committees (s. 57)
- extending boundaries (s. 86.1)
- exceptions regarding successor board determinations (s. 135)
- new district school boards, elections, transfers, powers and procedures of the Education Improvement Commission (ss. 58.1, 58.2)
- school councils (s. 170(3))
- class size (s. 170.1(5))
- teacher assistants (s. 170.3)
- agreements by boards for joint services (s. 171.1)
- school authority honoraria (s. 191.1(3))
- land reserved as school sites (s. 195(7))[23]
- electronic meetings (s. 208.1)
- school board estimates (s. 232)
- legislative and municipal grants (s. 234)
- investments by school boards (s. 241)
- debt limits of school boards (s. 242)
- borrowing by school boards and reserve funds (s. 247(3))
- a provincial financial services agency to school boards (s. 248)
- taxes generally (s. 257)
- tax rates (s. 257.12)
- tax notices (ss. 257.14(1), 257(27))
- tax collection (s. 257.19)
- education development charges (s. 257.10)
- Ontario education numbers (s. 266.5(1))
- terms and conditions of employment for principals and vice-principals (s. 287.1(2))

The court challenge to the delegations of power in Bill 160 was not to individual items of delegated power but rather was to the fact that the cumula-

---

[23] This section has not yet been proclaimed.

tive effect of the delegations in Bill 160 was inconsistent with the system of law-making by an elected body contemplated by the Constitution. Cumming J. upheld the delegations of power, concluding that:

> While one can appreciate the applicants' references to the rule of law, and to the possibility that the regulation-making powers entrusted to the government by Bill 160 are indeed very extensive, the statutory provisions fulfill the necessary procedural requirements, which is all this Court may assess. The objects of the sections authorizing regulations are ascertainable, and there is accordingly a basis for legal debate.[24]

The judge went further and held that even the power to tax and to set tax rates can be delegated to the executive, so long as the delegation is "express".[25]

This approach is consistent with the decision of the Divisional Court in 1986 in the challenge to the interim regulations which, prior to the enactment of Bill 30, authorized the extension of funding to Roman Catholic secondary schools.[26] The court there held that the regulation-making power conferred on the executive was sufficiently broad to enable it to accomplish this kind of change to the publicly funded system. The conclusion to be drawn from the decisions referred to is that for a purported delegation of power to be held invalid there must be an abdication of power by the legislature, that is, if a statute provided that "the Lieutenant Governor in Council may make such regulations in relation to education as he or she sees fit".

---

[24] *Bill 160 Case* (1998), 162 D.L.R. (4th) 257 at p. 327(Ont. Ct. (Gen. Div.)), appeal allowed in part 172 D.L.R. (4th) 193 (C.A.).

[25] For the scope of the power to tax which may be exercised by regulation, see Chapter 10, "New Funding Model: Tax Revenue".

[26] *Metropolitan Toronto School Board v. Minister of Education* (1986), 27 D.L.R. (4th) 47 (Ont. Div. Ct.).

3

Provincial Agencies

There are three kinds of provincial bodies which can be set up in Ontario for particular purposes. Two of these are appointed by the government or the Minister under powers conferred by the *Education Act* or the *Public Inquiries Act*[1] and exist for a limited period of time. The third is set up by legislation.

First, there are commissions of inquiry, sometimes called Royal Commissions, to "inquire into and report upon any school matter", usually of a comprehensive nature.[2] Examples are the Royal Commission on Education in Ontario (the Hope Commission) in 1950; the Commission on the Financing of Elementary and Secondary Education in Ontario in 1985 (the Macdonald Commission), and the Royal Commission on Learning in 1994. These commissions have the powers of a commission under Part II of the *Public Inquiries Act*.[3]

Secondly, the Minister can appoint advisory or consultative bodies to advise and report on specific issues. Recent exercises of this power followed the announcement by the Minister in May, 1997, of a new approach to education funding in Ontario — student-focused funding. As part of the announcement of student-focused funding, the Minister appointed teams of specialists to provide to the government technical advice in four key areas: pupil accommodation, learning opportunities grants, special education grants, and financial reporting and accountability. The panels were given three months in which to submit final reports to the Minister. They did so and then ceased to exist.

The third type of body is created by legislation, usually by statute but occasionally by regulation, with duties of a continuing nature. Such bodies exist until repeal of the statute or revocation of the regulation which created them. These bodies are primarily advisory but some have powers of decision and enforcement of those decisions. It is these institutions which are part of the governance structure of education.

---

[1] R.S.O. 1990, c. P.41.

[2] *Education Act*, s. 10.

[3] Including the powers to summon witnesses, to require witnesses to produce documents and give evidence on oath or affirmation, and to apply to the court to have witnesses cited for contempt.

EDUCATION IMPROVEMENT COMMISSION

The Education Improvement Commission (EIC) was set up originally under Bill 104 to "oversee the transition to the new system of education governance in Ontario".[4] For this broad purpose, the EIC was given powers during the transition period to:

- provide for the transfer by regulation of assets, liabilities and employees to the new boards, and ensure that assets were not unduly diminished pending transfer
- monitor the actions of existing boards to ensure their compliance with the new regime, and review, approve, change and monitor 1997 budgets
- exercise transitional control over existing boards' financial and property transactions, agreements, and hiring and promotion of staff
- perform audits and require the production of documents and information
- appoint auditors with broad powers of inquiry
- issue orders and directives which were immune from court review for the exercise of delegated powers
- enforce its orders as if they were court orders and apply for court enforcement of other orders

The broad scope of these powers provoked court challenges, primarily by public school boards and teacher federations, on a number of grounds.[5] Objections and arguments included:

1. The very wide powers of delegation and subdelegation conferred on the commission subjected elected trustees to the decisions of delegates of appointed officials and to the delegates of their delegates.
2. There were virtually no discernible standards by which commission processes would be carried out.
3. There was no general requirement on the commission to act fairly, reasonably, equitably or in the public interest.
4. There was a lack of legal controls or statutory guidelines on the commission and it was exempted from the usual procedural fairness requirements and the machinery of public accountability established for the exercise of delegated powers.

---

[4] *Education Act*, s. 335(2).
[5] *See, e.g., Bill 104 Case* (1997), 151 D.L.R. (4th) 346 (Ont. Ct. (Gen. Div.)).

The judge who heard the court challenge said that he was:

> . . . unable to accept the proposition that the cumulative provisions of the Act, standing by themselves, demonstrate any actual present violation of the rule of law in relation to procedural values . . . If the government or the commission or its agents violate the rule of law, the time to challenge that violation is when it occurs.[6]

The EIC was able to accomplish its purposes and survive the transitional period without resort to its extensive enforcement powers. The judgment on Bill 104 was rendered in August, 1997. Bill 160, which received Royal Assent in December, 1997, repealed most of the provisions to which objection had been made. At the same time, Cabinet made a regulation establishing in detail a process for the transfer of assets, liabilities and employees to the new boards, with extensive procedures for the resolution of disputes.[7] Under the regulation and Bill 160, the EIC retained its general role in the transition but its role was more specifically defined and procedurally circumscribed.

The other role of the EIC is an advisory one to the Minister. It is empowered to make recommendations to the Minister on French-language boards, the representation of Indians on boards, the out-sourcing of non-instructional services by boards, the role of school councils, increasing parental involvement in education governance and any other key issues which it believes should be addressed.[8] To date the EIC has published three reports.[9]

The Act provides that the term of office of the members of the commission will end on December 31, 2000.[10]

EDUCATION QUALITY AND ACCOUNTABILITY OFFICE

The Education Quality and Accountability Office was set up by the government in 1996 as a Crown Agency[11] to evaluate quality and effectiveness of elementary and secondary school education.[12] To this end, the office is to:

---

[6] *Bill 104 Case, supra*, at p. 361.

[7] *Transition from Old Boards to District School Boards*, O. Reg. 460.97 (as amended to O. Reg. 477/98).

[8] *Education Act*, s. 335(3).

[9] *The Road Ahead: A Report on Learning Time, Class Size and Staffing* (Education Improvement Commission, August, 1997); *A Report on the Role of School Boards* (Education Improvement Commission, December, 1997); *The Road Ahead III: A Report on the Role of School Councils* (Education Improvement Commission, November, 1998).

[10] Section 334(4.1).

[11] Under the *Crown Agency Act*, R.S.O. 1990, c. C.48, s. 2, a Crown agency is "for all its purposes an agent of Her Majesty and its powers may be exercised only as an agent of Her Majesty" (*i.e.*, the Government of Ontario).

[12] The office was created by the *Education Quality and Accountability Office Act*, 1996, S.O. 1996, c. 11 (as amended to 1997, c. 31).

- develop and require the administering and marking of tests of pupils
- develop systems for evaluating the quality and effectiveness of education
- research the schools' conduct on assessing academic achievement
- report and make recommendations to the public and to the Minister specifically on the results of tests and generally on the quality and effectiveness of school education and the public accountability of boards[13]

The office can require boards to administer tests to pupils in their schools, mark the tests and report on the results to the office and the general public within the jurisdiction of the board.[14] It can also require a board to provide information to the office,[15] including "personal information" within the meaning of s. 38 of the *Freedom of Information and Protection of Privacy Act*[16] and s. 28 of the *Municipal Freedom of Information and Protection of Privacy Act*.[17] Boards must comply with the directives of the office and pupils must take any test directed to be administered to them.[18]

The Minister can issue written directives and establish policies on matters relating to the objects of the office and delegate to the board of directors any of the Minister's powers and duties.[19] The board of directors can in turn delegate any of those powers and duties to the executive director who can delegate them to an employee of the office.[20]

The office is managed by its board of directors, composed of a minimum of seven and a maximum of nine directors appointed by Cabinet for fixed terms.[21]

The office makes an annual report to the Minister which is tabled in the Legislative Assembly.[22]

Cabinet can make regulations on specified matters relating to the office and on "any matter that the Lieutenant Governor in Council considers necessary or advisable to carry out effectively the intent and purpose of [the] Act".[23]

Before a regulation is made, the Minister is to consult with the office about it,[24] but no regulations have yet been made.

---

[13] *Education Quality and Accountability Office Act, 1996*, s. 3.
[14] Section 4.
[15] Section 9(6).
[16] R.S.O. 1990, c. F.31 (as amended to 1998, c. 26).
[17] R.S.O. 1990, c. M.56 (as amended 1997, c. 25).
[18] *Education Quality and Accountability Office Act*, s. 4(5), (6).
[19] Sections 6(1), 8(1).
[20] Section 16(3), (4).
[21] Section 11.
[22] Section 25.
[23] Section 26(1).
[24] Section 26(2).

LANGUAGES OF INSTRUCTION COMMISSION OF ONTARIO

The language of instruction in Ontario schools operated by school authorities[25] is governed by Part XII of the *Education Act*, "Language of Instruction". The function of the Languages of Instruction Commission of Ontario established under the *Education Act* is to consider issues relating to minority language instruction by school authorities referred to it by either a French-language rights holders' group or by the Minister. A group of 10 French-language rights holders of a school authority may develop a proposal to meet the educational and cultural needs of the French-speaking persons who are resident pupils of the school authority and of the French-speaking community served by the school authority.

The school authority must consider any proposal that is submitted in writing and cannot refuse to approve it without giving the group an opportunity to be heard.

If a school authority approves a proposal, it gives notice of the approval to the Minister, together with a recommendation that a regulation be made implementing it. A school authority that refuses to approve such a proposal must, within 30 days after receiving the proposal, forward to the group written reasons for the refusal. The French-language rights holders' group is then entitled to refer the issue to the commission.

If the commission considers that the proposal could be conducive to meeting the educational and cultural needs of the minority community (French-speaking or English-speaking), it must refer it to mediation. Otherwise, the commission takes no action.

If mediation fails, the commission itself must consider the matter and make recommendations, which the school authority can accept or reject.

If the school authority rejects the recommendation, it must given written reasons. The commission then must reconsider the issue and make a report and recommendation to the Minister.

The power of decision resides in the Minister, who can order the school authority, the commission, or both, to take such action as the Minister considers appropriate. The Minister's order can be filed with the Superior Court of Justice and enforced as an order of the court.

The Minister can also refer to the commission any matter relating to instruction in the French language or, where the pupils of a school authority who

---

[25] See *Education Act*, s. 1, for definition of "school authority" (which includes boards of district school areas, boards of rural separate schools, boards of combined separate school zones, boards of secondary school districts established by Cabinet in territorial districts, boards established by the Minister on Crown lands and boards of Protestant separate schools, as also defined by the *Education Act*). For definition of terms, see Chapter 4 under heading "Terminology".

receive instruction in the English language are a minority of the pupils of the school authority, any matter relating to instruction in the English language. The commission must refer to mediation any matter referred to it and the same process described previously is followed.

ONTARIO PARENT COUNCIL

The Ontario Parent Council was first established by the *Education Act* in 1993[26] and is composed of not more than 18 members appointed by the Minister. A member must be a parent or guardian of a child enrolled in an elementary or secondary school in Ontario.

Members of the council are appointed for a term of two years and may be reappointed for further terms but no member can be appointed for three or more consecutive terms.

The Minister designates the chair from among the members of the council. The members of the council may be paid remuneration and expenses as determined by Cabinet. The Ministry provides the council with staff and accommodation.

The statutory obligation of the council is to advise the Minister on issues related to elementary and secondary school education and methods of increasing parental involvement in elementary and secondary school education.

The council reports on its activities annually to the Minister. The report published by the council for 1997-98 indicates that members devoted much of their time to the development of the revised elementary curriculum in the areas of arts, language, French as a second language, mathematics, science and technology, physical and health education, and social studies. The council members were involved in the development of the secondary school curriculum through their participation on the subject panels established by the Ministry, to provide guidance and recommendations to the writers of the curriculum documents.

The council met with the Minister and with a number of agencies, such as the Education Improvement Commission, the Ontario College of Teachers and the Education Quality and Accountability Office, as well as with senior officials and staff of the Ministry, to discuss and provide input into education reform initiatives.

The council participated as a member of the Assessment Advisory Committee of the Education Quality and Accountability Office. The council presented a brief to the Social Development Standing Committee of the Legislature on Bill 160 and made a presentation to the Standing Committee on Finance and Economic Affairs on the pre-budget consultations.

---

[26] Section 17.1.

A newsletter outlining major areas of education reform, curriculum, assessment, report cards and school councils was published in March, 1998, and circulated to parents through the schools.

There is no formal relationship between the Ontario Parent Council and the school councils.[27] Only the parent council has direct access to the Ministry. School councils operate on the local level while the Ontario Parent Council operates on the provincial level.

The Education Improvement Commission has advised the Ministry that school councils should have input into decisions made by the Ministry and other provincial bodies, the Education Quality and Accountability Office and the Ontario College of Teachers. The EIC has also recommended that:

(a) the Ministry restructure the council into a provincial body that represents the province's school councils;

(b) the new organization consist of parents elected by school councils;

(c) the membership be representative of all four publicly funded systems and the geographic regions of the province; and

(d) the Ministry and its agencies seek the advice of the restructured Ontario Parent Council on those issues that fall within the responsibilities of school councils.[28]

The new organization would not duplicate school boards or other administrative structures. It should have two roles: providing advice to the Minister; and helping school councils share best practices.

EDUCATION RELATIONS COMMISSION

Under the *School Boards and Teachers Collective Negotiations Act*,[29] the Education Relations Commission had extensive powers in collective bargaining between school boards and the teachers' federations, and the resolution and arbitration of disputes. The Act, however, was repealed by Bill 160.

The commission continues to exist but for the limited purposes of:

(a) advising Cabinet when the continuation of a strike or lock-out or the closing of a school or schools is likely to place in jeopardy the successful completion of courses of study by pupils;

(b) making determinations on bargaining in good faith in respect of applications made before January 1, 1998; and

---

27 For discussion of school councils, see Chapter 8 under heading "School Councils".

28 See *The Road Ahead III: A Report on the Role of School Councils* (Education Improvement Commission, November, 1998).

29 R.S.O. 1990, c. S.2 (repealed 1997, c. 31, s. 178).

(c) compiling statistical information on the supply, distribution, professional activities and salaries of teachers.

In all other respects, teachers collective bargaining is now under the jurisdiction of the Ontario Labour Relations Board.[30]

PROVINCIAL SCHOOLS AUTHORITY

The Provincial Schools Authority, constituted under the *Provincial Schools Negotiations Act*,[31] is the employer of the principals, vice-principals and teachers in provincial schools, that is, schools operated by the Ministry of the Solicitor General and Correctional Services, the Ministry of Education and Training or the Ministry of Health.

The authority consists of five members appointed by Cabinet and is responsible for all matters relating to the employment of teachers. For this purpose, the authority has all the powers of and is subject to the duties and liabilities of a public school board under the Act.

The jurisdiction of the authority is limited as administration of the schools and teachers is the responsibility of a deputy minister of the Ministry which operates the school. However, in the event of a strike against or a lock-out by the authority, the authority can close a school if it is of the opinion that:

(a) the safety of pupils might be endangered during the strike or lock-out;
(b) the school building or the equipment or supplies in the building might not be adequately protected during the strike or lock-out; or
(c) the strike or lock-out will substantially interfere with the operation of the school.

The authority must have the consent of the Minister administering the school for a lock-out or school closing.

PROVINCIAL SCHOOL ATTENDANCE COUNSELOR

The Provincial School Attendance Counselor is appointed by Cabinet under authority conferred by the Act, with power under the direction of the Minister to "superintend and direct the enforcement of compulsory school attendance".[32]

---

[30] *Education Act*, s. 277.12.
[31] R.S.O. 1990, c. P. 35 (as amended to 1997, c. 31).
[32] *Education Act*, s. 24.

Every board must appoint a school attendance officer and notify the Provincial School Attendance Counselor of the appointment. The school attendance counselor is responsible for the enforcement of compulsory school attendance of every child who is required to attend school and who is a qualified resident pupil of the board or who has been enrolled in a school operated by the board. The school attendance counselor has the same powers with respect to pupils who are in a program of supervised alternative learning for excused pupils.

The Provincial School Attendance Counselor has all the powers of a school attendance counselor and can exercise those powers anywhere in Ontario. The Provincial School Attendance Counselor is obliged to hold an inquiry into the validity of a reason or excuse asserted by a parent or guardian for a child's non-attendance at school if the counselor believes that the child should not be excused. The counselor appoints a person or persons other than employees of the relevant board to conduct a hearing and report the result of the inquiry to the counselor. The counselor can then by written order direct that the child either attend school or be excused from attendance.

The counselor must also direct an inquiry if requested to do so by a court in a proceeding against a parent or guardian for failing to ensure a child's attendance at school without legal excuse. In these circumstances, the counselor reports to the court on the validity of the excuse rather than making an order.

The other principal duty of the counselor arises if a board is not providing accommodation or instruction for its resident pupils or has in other respects failed to comply with the Act and the regulations, or if the election of members of the board has been neglected and no regular board is in existence. In any of these situations, the Minister can direct the Provincial School Attendance Counselor to ensure the provision and maintenance of accommodation and instruction for pupils and generally that schools be established, maintained and conducted in accordance with the Act and the regulations. Thereupon, the Provincial School Attendance Counselor has for the period authorized by the Minister all the authority and powers vested in the board. The board is, in effect, placed under the trusteeship of the counselor.

ONTARIO COLLEGE OF TEACHERS

The Ontario College of Teachers is part of the governance structure of education, as it regulates the teaching profession and governs the members of the profession. The college was established as a corporate body by a statute passed in 1996 and is administered by the Minister.[33] The college is empowered to:

---

[33] *Ontario College of Teachers Act, 1996*, S.O. 1996, c. 12 (as amended to 1997, c. 31).

- establish qualifications for membership in the college and accredit professional and ongoing education programs for teachers offered by post-secondary educational institutions
- govern certificates of qualification and registration
- establish and enforce professional standards and ethical standards for teachers
- investigate complaints against teachers and deal with discipline and fitness-to-practice issues
- provide and accredit educational programs leading to certificates of additional qualification, including certificates of qualification as a supervisory officer

The governing body of the college is its council which consists of 17 members of the college elected by the members and 14 members appointed by Cabinet. The registrar is the chief executive officer and secretary of the council of the college, and participates as a member of the council (but without a vote). The council has an executive committee and committees for specific purposes, including investigation, discipline, and fitness-to-practice and registration appeals, all of which are known as "statutory committees".

The Investigation Committee considers and investigates complaints about the conduct or actions of a member of the college made by a member of the public, the college, the registrar or the Minister.

The Discipline Committee holds hearings on complaints of professional misconduct or incompetence referred to it by the Investigation Committee, the council or the executive committee, and on applications for reinstatement and removal of suspensions referred to it by the registrar.

The Fitness to Practice Committee hears and determines matters of capacity. If the committee finds that a member is suffering from a physical or mental condition or a disorder such that the member is unfit to continue to carry out his or her professional responsibilities, it may revoke or suspend a certificate or make it subject to terms, conditions or limitations.

The Registration Appeals Committee hears requests for the review of decisions of the registrar to refuse to issue a certificate of qualification and registration, or to impose terms, conditions or limitations on a certificate of qualification and registration to which an applicant has not consented.

There is a right of appeal to the Ontario Divisional Court on questions of law or fact, or both, against any decision or order of these committees. The court can affirm or rescind the decision of the committee appealed from, exercise all powers of the committee, direct the committee to take any action which the committee has power to take, substitute its opinion for that of the committee or refer the matter back to the committee for rehearing, in whole or in part.

The council, subject to Cabinet approval and prior review by the Minister, has extensive powers to make regulations and can also make by-laws with respect to "the administrative and domestic affairs" of the college.[34]

Regulations have been made under the Act by Cabinet governing the first election of members of the council, transitional discipline matters, appointments to the council by Cabinet, the composition and procedures of the statutory committees, teachers' qualifications and acts which constitute professional misconduct.[35]

PLANNING AND IMPLEMENTATION COMMISSION

This commission was set up by Bill 30 in 1986 to "advise the Minister in respect of specific means by which the extension of the Roman Catholic school system to include secondary school education may best be carried out".[36] The commission evaluated the plans of Roman Catholic and public boards in relation to the extension of the Roman Catholic system and its effect on employment and school properties.

The Act enabled the commission to arrange and assist in negotiations among boards for the transfer of school properties, and to recommend to the Minister the appointment of mediators to assist boards to reach agreement on issues in disputes. The Minister had the power to appoint a tribunal to hear and decide issues which could not otherwise be resolved.[37]

After the controversy resulting from the decision of a tribunal in the City of Hamilton, issues were thereafter resolved by negotiation and mediation with intervention by the Ministry when needed to provide financial inducements to boards to arrive at agreements. Generally, however, the role and impact of the commission in the reduction of the problems resulting from Bill 30 and their highly charged political content was minimal. The gravity of the fundamental changes which Bill 30 brought about required the direct involvement of the political actors, school boards, the Ministry and public opinion.

---

[34] *Ontario College of Teachers Act, 1996*, s. 41.
[35] *First Election*, O. Reg. 344/96 (revoked September 1, 1997 (O. Reg. 334/96, s. 34)); *Transitional Matters — Discipline*, O. Reg. 276/97; *Appointments to Council*, O. Reg. 345/96; *General*, O. Reg. 72/97; *Teachers Qualifications*, O. Reg. 184/97; *Professional Misconduct*, O. Reg. 437/97.
[36] *Education Act*, s. 148(1).
[37] Sections 148-153.

4

School Boards

INTRODUCTION

An understanding of the development of the education system in the 19th century is important for a number of reasons. In fact, it is essential for an appreciation of the constitutional and legal mandates which must still be observed by the legislature and government in the formulation of policy changes. Many of the aspects of Bill 160 which may at first sight appear to be short on reason or logic are explained by a need to avoid constitutional pitfalls.

The values which were the foundation of the development of the system are important because they worked in practice and it is often no answer to those skeptical of changes to say that we now inhabit a different world. That we live in a different world from Descartes and Gallileo does not invalidate their insights of mind and science.

Those who participate in the debates on change need to know the reasons for their passions, the values which they are expressing, the restraints which reform is bound to observe, the answers to the questions which must be asked:

- Why do we have school boards?
- Do we have to have school boards?
- Do we have to have separate school boards?
- What are the options for minority language education?
- What is the importance of local taxation and designation of support for the different kinds of boards?
- What are the limits of provincial intervention?
- Can the province dictate how school boards spend the money they raise locally, how much they can raise and when they can hire?
- What is the permissible and most effective distribution of power among the province, provincial agencies, trustees, superintendents, pupils, parents and ratepayers?

BASIS OF LOCAL GOVERNANCE

Authority, power and influence in education governance have from the province's beginnings been a shared exercise, between central authority and local government.[1] In the early part of the 19th century, local institutions were the dominant partner.

The values which inspired the development of the school systems in Upper Canada in the 19th century were local effort, local voluntary action, self-management, self-government and local "home rule". These values were expressed and implemented by school boards in co-operation with the central authority but with exclusive control over many aspects of governance, including revenue locally raised, residing in the boards. These concepts were constantly emphasized by Egerton Ryerson in his reports on education and reflected in the legislation which he largely drafted himself from 1846 to 1871. Commenting on the recent comprehensive reforms effected by statute in 1846 and 1847,[2] Ryerson wrote that:

> . . . the entire efficiency of [the school law] . . . with the bare exception of the apportionment of the Legislative grant, depends upon the voluntary action of the people themselves, in their local district or school section municipalities, or isolated or domestic and individual relations.[3]

Ryerson envisioned this voluntary action as expressed by the essential role of local government in the province's educational affairs.

Commenting on the Act of 1847 extending the rights of cities and towns, he wrote that:

> . . . the same reasons which justify the incorporation of cities and towns for the more efficient management of their local affairs, and the promotion of their local interests generally, require a like incorporation of their public school system for the best interests of the rising generation.[4]

In an "explanatory paper", "The Public Voice on the Present System of Elementary Education in Upper Canada", in 1848, Ryerson underlined the necessity of the local management of schools:

> The education of the people through themselves is the vital principle of the law. Coercion is alien to the spirit of the system. It is essentially a system of voluntary development; and the very administration of it, in the various Municipalities and School Sections, has been a species of social Normal training, eminently conducive to the diffusion of a spirit of self-reliance, intelligence and patriotic enterprise.[5]

---

[1] See discussion in Chapter 2 under heading "Partnership".

[2] *Common Schools Act*, S.U.C. 1846, c. 20; *Common Schools Act*, S.U.C. 1847, c. 19.

[3] *Annual Report* (Ontario Department of Education, 1847).

[4] *Ibid.*, at p. 77.

[5] See J.G. Hodgins, *Documentary History of Education in Upper Canada from the*

In his annual report for 1857, Ryerson wrote:

> . . . our school system is one of mutual co-operation between the Government
> and the people in each municipality. The Act of Parliament defines the objects to
> be accomplished, the parties to act, the assistance to be given; the Council of
> Public Instruction prepares rules to carry into effect the provisions of the law . . .
> and the Chief Superintendent sees that the conditions of the law are fulfilled.
>
> But nothing can be done in any municipality without the co-operation of the
> people in their collective or national capacity, and in accordance with their
> wishes — their school affairs being under their own management. Thus the
> school system, as is the municipal system, is a training school of local self-gov-
> ernment to the freeholders and householders in each municipality, while it is the
> potent instrument of educating their children.[6]

In his annual report for 1858, Ryerson wrote of the recently established
separate school system and the taxation and managerial rights of separate
school trustees:

> Having settled the principles and created the framework of the School System
> and secured inviable parental supremacy and the rights of conscience in all mat-
> ters of religion, the Legislature transferred the responsibility and power of man-
> agement to parents and rate-payers themselves in each municipality.[7]

The vehicle for this "responsibility and power of management" was the local school board. A respected education historian has stated unequivocally:

> The cornerstone of the system of publicly funded education in Canada West and
> Ontario has always been the local school board. It was and is the institution
> charged with the administration of schools. School boards have always been
> composed of individuals elected from among the qualified school supporters to
> represent the parents and community in carrying out the task of educating their
> children.[8]

Ryerson was firm that school boards were autonomous with respect to the
revenue they raised themselves, and that provincial powers did not extend to
interfering with local school expenditures:

> . . . I may remark that his statements in the latter part of the extract enclosed by
> you [Provincial Secretary A.N. Morin] are without foundation, and are contrary
> to fact, as I have for years past, in various official communications to school
> authorities in different municipalities (and not all in reference to Separate
> Schools) stated, that I had no authority to interfere in the expenditure of moneys

---

Passing of the Constitutional Act of 1791 to the Close of Dr. Ryerson's Administration of the Education Department in 1876, vol. VIII (1848-49), p. 287.

[6] *Annual Report* (Ontario Department of Education, 1857), p. 38.

[7] See "The Chief Superintendent's Annual Report for 1858" in J.G. Hodgins, ed.,
Historical Education Papers and Documents of Ontario, 1842-1861, vol. V
(Toronto, King's Printer, 1912), pp. 261-2.

[8] Affidavit of Dr. R. Dixon, filed as evidence (at p. 77) in *Daly v. Ontario (Attorney
General)* (1997), 154 D.L.R. (4th) 464 (Ont. Ct. (Gen. Div.)), affd 172 D.L.R. (4th)
241 (C.A.).

raised by municipalities for school purposes, beyond the amounts they were required by law to provide — that they could apply such monies by in giving
additional aid to Common Schools, Separate or Public, as they might judge expe-
dient, the principle of local self-government, with no other than a few essential
limitations forming the basis of the municipal system of Upper Canada.[9]

This principle has received recent judicial affirmation in Alberta:

> The constitutional imperatives dictate the result: the [provincial] *Framework* re-
> strictions do not apply to any funds raised by opted-out separate schools through
> taxation of their supporters. The Government is precluded from withholding
> grants from separate boards that do not comply with the *Framework's* conditions
> *relative to locally requisitioned funds.*[10]

Until Bill 104 and Bill 160, this was both the law and the practice in Ontario.

EDUCATION AS PUBLIC GOOD

It has been emphatically stated that:

> . . . over the 200-year sweep of our educational history — from the 1790s to the
> 1990s — no decade was so fertile, so creative, and so decisive, as that of the
> 1840s. A succession of statutes between 1841 and 1850 established the legal
> framework of the Upper Canadian common school system, one that in its most
> essential features would remain unaltered for decades to come.[11]

The common schools were public institutions, administered by trustees elected
by all of the ratepayers within a particular area. The schools were local institutions, governed by elected representatives of local people and accessible to all
children of ratepayers resident in that locality.

The principle of local tax support for local schools was well established.
Government grants contributed to educational finance but the schools were
supported primarily by local property taxes levied by municipal institutions.

The principle of shared policy-making and administrative responsibility between the central and the local community was also an established one and a
rudimentary but adequate organizational structure existed at both levels of government. After the 1847 Act, urban boards ran their own systems and they
became leaders in the provincial educational system.

---

[9] E. Ryerson to A.N. Morin, April 17, 1852: see *The Roman Catholic Bishop of
Toronto and the Chief Superintendent of Schools on the Subject of Separate Common Schools in Upper Canada* (Quebec, John Lovell, 1852).

[10] *Public School Boards' Assn. of Alberta v. Alberta (Attorney General)* (1998), 158
D.L.R. (4th) 267, supplementary reasons 163 D.L.R. (4th) 275 (Alta. C.A.), *per*
Berger J.A., at p. 328.

[11] Professor Robert Gidney in sworn evidence (affidavit, at p. 14) in the *Bill 160 Case*
(1998), 162 D.L.R. (4th) 257 (Ont. Ct. (Gen. Div.)), appeal allowed in part 172
D.L.R. (4th) 193 (C.A.).

The decision to finance the education system exclusively through property taxation was to acknowledge that education was a public rather than a private good and that public benefits should be financed by the entire community or, as Ryerson put it repeatedly, it meant "a tax upon the property of all, by the majority, for the education of all". In Upper Canada, the systems were run "not by legislation imposed by the state, but by the decision of the voters in every school section in the province, and by locally elected trustees in the urban areas".[12]

GRAMMAR SCHOOL BOARDS

The first legislation for the establishment and funding of schools in Upper Canada was the *Act to establish Public Schools in each and every District of this Province* of 1807.[13] The schools which it established were called "public schools" but, as these schools eventually became the "grammar schools", the legislation has become known as the *"Grammar Schools Act"*.

This legislation established public schools in each of eight districts in the province and a board of trustees for each district and provided for an annual grant of £100 for each school for payment of teachers' salaries. In 1819 these schools were renamed district schools and in 1839 were again renamed, this time as grammar schools.

Under the Act of 1807, trustees for grammar schools were appointed by the province. Local participation in the selection of trustees for grammar schools did not begin until 1853. The 1853 Act provided for trustees appointed by the municipal council of a county or union of counties.

Grammar schools were integrated into the common school system and brought under the authority of the Council of Public Instruction, the Chief Superintendent, and county or city councils. In 1871, they became "high schools", the genesis of what are now defined in the *Education Act* as "secondary schools".

COMMON SCHOOL BOARDS

Common school trustees, on the other hand, were from the beginning elected to their position directly by the inhabitants. The first legislation in Upper Canada with respect to common schools was the *Common Schools Act* of 1816.[14] This Act was passed to establish common schools in every district in

---

[12] *Ibid.*, at p. 22. See also E. Ryerson, "Address to the Inhabitants of Upper Canada", in *Annual Report* (Ontario Department of Education, 1849, No. 6), p. 46.

[13] S.U.C. 1807, c. 6.

[14] S.U.C. 1816, c. 36.

the province, with an annual provincial grant of £6000 paid to and disbursed by the district treasurer.

A competent group of persons within a district could build or provide a school house for not less than 20 students, provide for part payment of the teacher's salary and appoint three persons to act as trustees of the common school with the power to appoint teachers. Effective power was exercised by the board of trustees for each district who were elected by the inhabitants.

Provincial participation was ensured by the grant to the province of the power and obligation to appoint from time to time not less than five persons to compose a board of education for each district, sometimes referred to as a district board, to report annually to the government. The trustees had the power to remove or dismiss teachers but only with the approval of the board of education for the district. The trustees were responsible for making the rules and regulations for the governing of the school subject to the approval of the board of education. Trustees had the right to sue to collect unpaid subscriptions and were required to report to the district board of education annually. With minor changes, the system established in 1816 continued in force until 1841.

The first comprehensive legislation was the *Common Schools Act* of 1841, passed by the United Province of Canada.[15] It provided for the election of five common school commissioners and introduced the concept of a local budget determined by the commissioners and raised by way of rates from the inhabitants by the district council which was also the board of education. This legislation was repealed in relation to Upper Canada and replaced in that province by the *Common Schools Act* of 1843,[16] which reintroduced the name "trustees" instead of "commissioners".

The trustees were constituted a body corporate with all the powers of a corporation except the right to hold property. They acquired this right in 1850. By 1859, trustees had acquired a range of powers which were to form the basis of local school board management until 1997.

The word "common" referred both to what was taught and who was taught. Before the 1840s, it did not imply anything about how the schools were administered, organized or financed. Some were state-funded; some were financed in other ways entirely.

In the early 19th century, a common school was any school that taught at least the rudiments of literacy and numeracy to the "common people". The term gradually aquired a number of meanings. It referred to "elementary schools" as opposed to grammar schools. It also came to be used to identify a state-funded school under the Common Schools Acts rather than one founded and maintained by voluntary means. It was also used to identify the public, non-denominational schools as contrasted with the separate, denominational

---

[15] S. Prov. Can. 1841, c. 18.
[16] S.U.C. 1843, c. 29.

schools, although separate schools were in law part of the common school system. The term was abandoned in 1871 and replaced by "public" school.

The word "public" retained the meanings previously ascribed to "common", so that "public schools" continued to be used in relation to elementary schools, publicly funded schools (as opposed to private schools) and non-denominational schools. In law, a "public school" is now a school, elementary or secondary, under the jurisdiction of a public board, so that "public" and "elementary" are no longer synonymous.[17] "Public district school board" means an English-language public district school board or a French-language public district school board.[18]

By 1859, common school trustees controlled the three essential elements of school governance: property, teachers and tax revenue. With respect to property, they had custody and safe keeping of all common school property and could acquire and hold land, moveable property, moneys or income for common school purposes and could build, repair, rent, warm, furnish and keep in order the school house, its furniture, appendages and lands.

The trustees also had the power to contract with and employ teachers and determine the amount of their salaries, and provide for the salaries of teachers and all other expenses of the school.

For revenue purposes, the trustees made out the list of ratepayers and the amount payable by each, and determined the method of payment. They required the local councils to levy and collect by rate according to the valuation of taxable property all amounts required for the support of the school, the purchase of school sites and the erection of school houses. They could exempt indigent persons from payment of the whole or part of school rates and charge the amount of the exemption upon other ratable inhabitants. They alone could collect, receive and account for all school moneys collected by rate-bill, subscription or otherwise from the inhabitants of the school section and could appoint a collector to collect the rates imposed by them upon the inhabitants.[19]

SEPARATE SCHOOL BOARDS

The first legislative provision for denominational schools was the *Common Schools Act* of 1841, which applied to both Upper and Lower Canada. That Act provided that, if a number of inhabitants professing a religious faith different from the majority of the inhabitants dissented, they could collectively elect a

---

[17] See definitions in *Education Act*, s. 1(1). See also discussion under heading "Termination", *infra*.

[18] For a complete description of the present nomenclature, see discussion under heading "Termination", *infra*.

[19] For a complete description of the revenue-raising tools, see Chapter 10, "New Funding Model: Tax Revenue".

trustee or trustees who had the same rights and obligations as the common school commissioners and establish and maintain a common school. Once established, the common school was entitled to receive its portion of the Common School Fund and amounts raised or levied by assessment for the support of common schools.

The 1841 Act was repealed in its application to Upper Canada by the *Common Schools Act* of 1843 which made the right of Protestants and Catholics to establish a separate school dependent upon the faith of the teacher of the common school rather than the faith of the majority of inhabitants.

The 1843 Act provided that if the common school teacher was Roman Catholic, at least 10 Protestant inhabitants were entitled to have a school with a teacher of their own "religious persuasion". At least 10 Roman Catholic inhabitants had the same right if the common school teacher was Protestant. The separate school was entitled to receive its share of the provincial grant according to the number of children of the religious persuasion attending the school. The separate schools were subject to the same visitations, conditions, rules and obligations as were other common schools.

The independent rights of Roman Catholics to establish separate schools and elect trustees for their management were created by the *Taché Act* of 1855.[20] Upon giving notice to the reeve or chairman of the board of common school trustees that trustees had been elected, five Roman Catholics constituted a board of trustees.

Every Roman Catholic separate school was entitled to a share of the annual grant by the legislature for the support of common schools on the basis of pupil attendance. In addition to a proportionate share of the provincial grant, separate schools were supported by taxation on the property of Roman Catholics who designated themselves as supporters of the separate school. The trustees of a Roman Catholic separate school had the power to impose, levy and collect school rates or subscriptions upon and from persons sending children to or subscribing towards the support of such schools and had all the powers in respect of separate schools that the trustees of common schools had under the provisions of the *Common Schools Act*.

Every person paying rates could give notice of being a Roman Catholic and separate school supporter and be exempt from payment of rates imposed for the support of common schools for the following year. Separate schools were not entitled to any part of school moneys arising from local assessment for common school purposes.

The decision about which means of finance to use was made at school meetings in the school sections and by the trustees themselves in urban areas. Like common school trustees, separate school trustees had the power to determine

---

[20] *Act to Amend the Laws relating to Separate Schools in Upper Canada*, S.U.C. 1855, c. 131.

the amount of money they deemed necessary. So long as the expenditures were lawful, there were no legal restrictions on the amount that they could levy for the separate schools.

Roman Catholic rights were further extended in 1863 by the *Scott Act*.[21] The election of trustees was now to be governed by the same provisions as for common school trustees and teachers were required to comply with the same provisions as the common school teachers. Trustees had the same powers as common school trustees.

School sections had the right to share in all legislative grants and not only the grant from the Common School Fund. Trustees were allowed to accept Roman Catholic students from outside of their school section.

The exemptions of support of common schools was extended from expenses of common schools and common school libraries to the purchase of land or erection of buildings for common school purposes.

Separate school supporters were no longer required to give annual notice of tax support; the notice remained in operation unless and until notice of withdrawal of support.

There were also separate schools for Protestants and "coloured persons". An application could be made to the municipal council of a township or to the common school board of an urban area by 12 Protestant or coloured heads of families for a separate Protestant or coloured school.

These schools were financed by subscriptions from their supporters equal to the taxes which would otherwise have been levied upon them in order to obtain the legislative grant for common schools. Protestant and coloured separate schools received a share of the legislative common school grant but were not entitled to any part of the moneys raised by local municipal assessment for common school purposes.

FRENCH-LANGUAGE BOARDS

Following adoption of s. 23 of the Charter and the decision of the Ontario Court of Appeal in *Reference re Education Act of Ontario and Minority Language Education Rights*,[22] the Ontario government established three different governance structures for French-language education. Every board was obliged to establish either a French-language advisory committee or a French-language section of the board.

Every board that had one or more resident pupils who exercised their right to receive instruction in a French-language instructional unit had to establish

---

[21] *Act to restore to Roman Catholics in Upper Canada certain rights in respect to Separate Schools*, S.U.C. 1863 (2nd Sess.), c. 5.

[22] (1984), 10 D.L.R. (4th) 491 (Ont. C.A.).

and operate one or more French-language instructional units for those pupils or enter into an agreement with another board to enable those pupils to receive instruction in a French-language instructional unit operated by the other board. Every board which operated a French-language "instructional unit" had to have a French-language section.

French-language sections within English-language school boards were composed of trustees elected to represent the French-language minority. They had exclusive jurisdiction in respect of matters affecting French-language instruction. Prior to Bill 104, there were 58 French-language sections. In 50 of these, the French-language community constituted a minority of the student population of the board.

In English-language boards without French-language sections, French-language advisory committees (FLAC) made recommendations to the board on matters respecting French-language education. FLACs lacked decision-making power.

The third option was French-language school boards, which were created by the government on an ad hoc basis in response to various pressures. Before 1998, the only independent French-language boards were in Metropolitan Toronto (Conseil des Écoles Françaises de la Communauté Urbaine de Toronto), Ottawa-Carleton (Conseil des Écoles Catholiques de Langue Française de la région d'Ottawa-Carleton, and Conseil des Écoles Publiques d'Ottawa-Carleton), and the County of Prescott and Russell (Conseil des Écoles Séparées Catholiques de Langue Française de Prescott-Russell).

Before Bill 104 and Bill 160, the French-speaking community had argued that there were unacceptable constraints imposed upon the administration of the public funds provided for French-language schools. The funds for French-language sections were allocated by the board and hence by the majority-language trustees rather than controlled by the French-language trustees on behalf of their constituents. FLACs were advisory bodies only. They had no power to make decisions on the expenditure of funds for French-language education. While the French-language school boards which did exist had control over their budgets, they did not have the tax base to raise revenue comparable to the resources available to English-language boards.

The most disadvantaged group was French-language Roman Catholics. Ratepayers who were entitled to designate their school taxes to a Roman Catholic French-language separate school board had to identify themselves as both Roman Catholic and French. Otherwise, their tax support went automatically to the English-language system. As a result, French-language schools did not receive the full extent of ratepayer support. Some French-language ratepayers failed to appreciate the importance of designating their support. Some failed to designate their support on a change of residence. Others had insufficient motivation to designate their support to the French-language school board because they had no children in the French-language system.

The French-speaking community had consistently argued that full management and control by the minority of French-language schools could only be achieved through the establishment of independent French-language school boards. The French-language community maintained that, given the number of minority language students in Ontario, a structure of minority language education governance was mandated by the Supreme Court of Canada's approach for determining entitlement under s. 23 of the Charter. Their claims were supported by the conclusions reached in the 1991 *Report of the French Language Education Governance Advisory Group*, the 1995 report of the Royal Commission on Learning[23] and the 1996 report of the Ontario School Board Reduction Task Force.[24]

There are now 12 French-language boards throughout the province, eight Roman Catholic and four public. Pupils who are not "French-speaking persons"[25] may be admitted to a school of a French-language board but such admission is under the control of the board. A request for admission of the pupil to a school of the board can be made to a French-language board by:

(a) the parent of a pupil who is not a French-speaking person;
(b) a person who has lawful custody of a pupil who is not a French-speaking person; or
(c) a pupil who is an adult and is not a French-speaking person.

The board can admit the pupil to one of its schools if the admission is approved by majority vote of an admissions committee appointed by the board and composed of:

(a) the principal of the school to which admission is requested;
(b) a teacher of the board; and
(c) a supervisory officer of the board.

There are similar provisions with respect to admission of such a pupil to a school of a school authority, except that in this case the admissions committee must be composed of:

---

[23] *For the Love of Learning* (Royal Commission on Learning, 1995).
[24] *Final Report* (Ontario School Board Reduction Task Force, 1996).
[25] Under the *Education Act*, a "French-speaking person" is a child of a person who has the right under the *Canadian Charter of Rights and Freedoms* to have his or her children receive their primary and secondary school instruction in the French language in Ontario regardless of the "where numbers warrant" provision in s. 23 of the Charter.

(a) the principal of the school to which admission is requested;

(b) a teacher who uses the French language in instruction in the school; and

(c) a French-speaking supervisory officer employed by the school authority or, if the school authority does not have one, one employed by another board or by the Ministry.[26]

TERMINOLOGY

Bill 104 and Bill 160 worked significant changes not only to the structure of governance but also to its terminology. For instance, terms which were in the *Education Act* before 1997 but which are no longer in use include:

- board of education
- public school board
- public school elector
- secondary school board
- Roman Catholic school board
- county combined separate school board
- district combined separate school board
- Protestant separate school board
- divisional board
- school division

Boards in existence before January 1, 1998, are now referred to as "old boards".

A "board" is now either a "district school board" or a "school authority". District school boards are organized as public or separate and as English-language or French-language. There are accordingly four kinds of district school boards:

(a) English-language public district school boards;

(b) English-language separate district school boards;

(c) French-language public district school boards; and

(d) French-language separate district school boards.

Boards

An "English-language public board" is either:

(a) an English-language public district school board; or

(b) a public school authority.

---

[26] See, generally, Part XII of the *Education Act*, "Language of Instruction".

An "English-language district school board" is either:

(a) an English-language public district school board; or
(b) an English-language separate district school board.

A "French-language district school board" is either:

(a) a French-language public district school board; or
(b) a French-language separate district school board.

An "English-language Roman Catholic board" is either:

(a) an English-language separate district school board; or
(b) a Roman Catholic school authority.

"Roman Catholic"

Three designations are used in the Act: "Roman Catholic"; "Catholic"; and "separate". In the section of the Act which provides for the establishment of district school boards, the term used is "separate district school boards". However, all boards which operate separate schools for Roman Catholics are named "Catholic district school boards", or "conseil scolaires de district catholique". This is the only use of the word "Catholic" or "catholique" standing alone. Before Bill 160, the term "Roman Catholic school board" was used in relation to separate school boards which had elected to provide secondary school education in accordance with Bill 30. That term is no longer in the Act. Instead, there is a new term, "Roman Catholic board".

"Roman" is not part of the name of any board but the term "Roman Catholic board" is used in the Act to refer to a "separate district school board" or a "Roman Catholic school authority". Thus, there is "Roman Catholic board", "Roman Catholic school authority" and "separate district school board".

"Separate school" remains in the Act to refer to a school under the jurisdiction of a Roman Catholic board. A school under the jurisdiction of a Roman Catholic school authority is a "rural separate school".

"Separate school board" also remains in the Act to refer to any board which operates a separate school for Roman Catholics but "separate" or "séparé" is not part of the name of any board.

"Roman Catholic" is not used in connection with French-language boards or board supporters, except that a French-language separate district school board is a "Roman Catholic board". "Roman Catholic" is not used in relation to district school boards but is used in relation to a supporter of an English-language separate district school board, an "English-language Roman Catholic board supporter", as this term includes district school boards and school authorities, "Roman Catholic boards".

In summary, a "separate district school board" is either:

(a) an English-language separate district school board; or
(b) a French-language separate district school board.

A "Roman Catholic board" is either:

(a) a separate district school board, French or English; or
(b) a Roman Catholic school authority.

A "Roman Catholic school authority" is either:

(a) a board of a rural separate school zone; or
(b) a board of a combined separate school zone.

"Public"

"Public" is simpler, subject to the fact that there is a distinction between "public board" and "public district school board".

A "public board" is:

(a) a public district school board; or
(b) a public school authority.

A "public district school board" is either:

(a) an English-language public district school board; or
(b) a French-language public district school board.

A "public school" is a school under the jurisdiction of a public board.
A "public school authority" is:

(a) a board of a district school area;
(b) a board of a secondary school district established by Cabinet in a territorial district ("s. 67 board"); or
(c) a board established by the Minister on Crown land ("s. 68 board").

A s. 67 board is a secondary school board established by Cabinet in an area in a territorial district which is not part of the area of jurisdiction of a public district school board.

A s. 68 board is a public board established by the Minister for elementary, secondary, or elementary and secondary school purposes on Crown lands, provincial or federal, which are exempt from taxation for school purposes.

"French-Language"

Persons

A "French-language rights holder" is a person who has the right under the *Canadian Charter of Rights and Freedoms* to have his or her children receive their primary and secondary school instruction in the French language in Ontario, regardless of the "where numbers warrant" provision. A "French-speaking person" is a child of a French-language rights holder.

A "French-language district school board supporter" is a French-language rights holder who is shown as a French-language public district school board supporter or as a French-language separate district school board supporter on the applicable school support list or who is declared to be such in a final decision in proceedings under the *Assessment Act.*[27]

Institutions

A "French-language instructional unit" is a class, group of classes or school in which the French-language or Quebec sign language is the language of instruction but does not include a class, group of classes or school of French immersion for English-speaking pupils.

A "French-language district school board" is a French-language public district school board or a French-language separate district school board, and can operate only classes and schools which are French-language instructional units.

"French-language sections" of boards and "French-language advisory committees" of boards no longer exist.

There is, of course, no defined English-language equivalent of "French-language rights holder" or "French-speaking person".

Board Support

The terminology described in the foregoing is also used in relation to board support.

An "English-language public board supporter" is defined, by exclusion, as a person who is an owner or tenant of residential property in the area of jurisdiction of a board and who is *not*:

(a) a separate school supporter;
(b) a French-language public district school board supporter; or
(c) a Protestant separate school board supporter.

---

[27] R.S.O. 1990, c. A.31 (as ameneded to 1998, c. 33).

Similarly for Roman Catholics, an English-speaking supporter of a Roman Catholic "board" is an "English-language Roman Catholic board supporter".

French-language rights holders are either a "French-language public district school board supporter" or a "French-language separate district school board supporter".

"District"

Bill 104 marked a return to a province-wide use of the appellation, "district". Before Bill 104, "district" was used only in relation to "district school area", "district combined separate school zone" and "district combined separate school board", which existed only in the territorial districts, mainly in Northern Ontario.

However, Upper Canada was first organized for municipal administration on the basis of large areas called "districts". For each district, there was a district board of education until they were abolished and districts were replaced by counties in the mid-19th century.

Thereafter, the basic unit of administration of education was the "school section", originally for common schools and separate schools. Later, the areas of jurisdiction of separate school boards were "separate school zones". Both of these terms are still in use. "School section" is confined to the area of jurisdiction of a public board for elementary school purposes only. There is no such limitation for "separate school zones".

The present form of territorial municipal organization consists of counties, regional municipalities and territorial districts. In the system of organization for education, "district" is used throughout the province. Every board in the province is a "district school board". The boards in the territorial districts are referred to as "school authorities".

However, a "district school area" is a school section in the territorial districts that is not a school section of a district school board or a school section designated as such by the Minister. Thus, "district" is retained in the territorial "districts", but only to define elementary school areas. It is not used for the "school authorities" in the territorial districts.

"District" is now used in the rest of the province to define school boards and the area in which a public board has jurisdiction for secondary school purposes, a "secondary school district".

"School Authorities" and "Education Authorities"

A "school authority" is:

(a) a board of a district school area;
(b) a board of a rural separate school;
(c) a board of a combined separate school zone;

    (d) a board of a secondary school district established under s. 67;

    (e) a board established under s. 68; or

    (f) a board of a Protestant separate school.

In the legislative grants regulations, school authorities other than s. 68 boards are called "isolate boards".

An "education authority" is a corporation that is incorporated by one or more bands or councils of bands for the purpose of providing for the educational needs of the members of the band or bands.

"Schools"

A "school" is:

    (a) the body of elementary school pupils or secondary school pupils that is organized as a unit for educational purposes under the jurisdiction of the appropriate board; or

    (b) the body of pupils enrolled in any of the elementary or secondary school courses of study in an educational institution operated by the Government of Ontario.

A school includes the teachers and other staff members associated with the unit or institution and the lands and premises used in connection with the unit or institution. Schools are either public schools or separate schools and either elementary schools or secondary schools.

A "public school" is a school under the jurisdiction of a public board.

A "separate school" is a school under the jurisdiction of a Roman Catholic board, except in the case of the one remaining Protestant separate school in the province (in Penetanguishine).

An "elementary school" is a school in which instruction is given in some or all of the primary division, junior division and intermediate division but not in the senior division.

A "secondary school" is a school in which instruction is given in some or all of the last two years of the intermediate division and the senior division.

A "private school" is one at which instruction is provided at any time between the hours of 9 a.m. and 4 p.m. on any school day for five or more pupils who are of or over compulsory school age in any of the subjects of the elementary or secondary school courses of study and that is not a school under the jurisdiction of a school board or school authority.

Schools are also maintained by the province for the blind and for the deaf. These schools are the responsibility of the Executive Director of the Regional Services Division of the Ministry.

Each school has a superintendent who may establish a superintendent's advisory council for his or her school to make recommendations to the superintendent on the organization, administration and government of the school.

The schools operate within a framework established by regulation.

"Trustees"

The term "trustee" has been replaced by "member of a board" but the Act allows a member of a board to be referred to as a trustee for all purposes of the Act.

5

Duties and Powers of School Boards

Every district school board is a corporation and has all the powers and must perform all the duties that are conferred or imposed on it under the Act or any other applicable statute or regulation.[1]

District school boards are creatures of statute and have, therefore, only the powers and duties conferred upon them. They are not corporations under the *Business Corporations Act*,[2] which have the capacity, rights, powers and privileges of a natural person.

Where a district school board is created by:

(a) one or more old boards being merged or amalgamated with a district school board to continue as a district school board;

(b) one or more school authorities being merged or amalgamated with a district school board to continue as a district school board; or

(c) two or more district school boards being merged or amalgamated to continue as a district school board,

the district school board which is thereby continued is a corporation.[3] The district school board possesses all the property, rights, privileges and franchises and is subject to all the liabilities, including civil, criminal and quasi-criminal, and all contracts, disabilities and debts of its predecessors. A conviction against or a ruling, order or judgment in favour of or against the predecessors can be enforced by or against the corporation. In any civil action commenced by or against the predecessors, the district school board becomes the plaintiff or defendant, as the case may be, in the proceeding.[4]

---

[1] *Education Act*, s. 58.5(1).

[2] R.S.O. 1990, c. B.16 (as amended to 1998, c. 18), s. 15.

[3] *Education Act*, s. 58.5(2).

[4] As a result of the express application to district school boards by s. 58.5(3) of the Act of s. 180(7) of the *Business Corporations Act*.

The Act confers on boards extensive but clearly defined duties and powers. There is a list of actions which a board must take as well as a list of activities which it may but is not obligated to undertake.

DUTIES OF BOARDS

The obligations of a board relate primarily to its administration, schools, teachers, instruction and textbooks, property and insurance.

A board must create and maintain a sound infrastructure by having a head office, appointing officers, ensuring payment of bills and establishing procedures for meetings.

Its main duty and function is to "provide instruction and adequate accommodation during each school year for the pupils who have a right to attend a school under the jurisdiction of a board" and to that end appoint for each school that it operates a principal and an adequate number of teachers, all of whom are members of the Ontario College of Teachers, and provide free the required textbooks.[5] Boards are also required to operate kindergartens and provide or ensure provision of special education programs and services.[6]

With respect to schools, a board must:

(i)   ensure that every school under its charge is conducted in accordance with the Act and the regulations;

(ii) keep its schools open during the whole period of the school year except where it is otherwise provided under the Act; and

(iii) keep the school buildings and premises in proper repair and in a proper sanitary condition, providing suitable furniture and equipment in proper repair, protecting the property of the board and ensuring adequate property and liability insurance.

Other obligations of a board are to notify the Minister of employees convicted of criminal offences of sexual misconduct involving minors or other offences that might pose a risk to pupils, to report to the Minister any children in their jurisdiction not enrolled in school, to transmit to the Minister all reports required by law and to establish school councils.[7]

Bill 160 introduced new obligations on boards with respect to class size[8] and teaching time.[9] Every board must now ensure that the average size of its

---

[5] *Education Act*, s. 170(1), paras. 6, 10, 12.

[6] Section 170(1), paras. 6.1, 7.

[7] Section 170(1).

[8] Section 170(1) (effective August 31, 1998).

[9] Section 170(1) (effective August 31, 1998). The total "instructional days" is governed by the *School Year Calendar*, O. Reg. 304 (as amended to O. Reg. 91/98).

elementary school classes, in the aggregate, does not exceed 25 pupils, and that of its secondary school classes, in the aggregate, does not exceed 22 pupils. The Minister, at the request of a board, may permit it to exceed these limits. A board determines the average size of its classes, in the aggregate, as of October 31 in each year. Every three years, the Minister must review the specified amounts of the maximum average class size.

A regulation has been made by Cabinet directing the method to be used by boards to determine average class size and outlining the obligations of directors of education for the preparation and distribution of annual reports on average class sizes.[10]

Amendments to the Act by Bill 160 also require that boards ensure that classroom teachers be in the classroom for the prescribed number of minutes in each week of the school year.[11] In the aggregate, elementary school classroom teachers must provide an average of at least 1300 minutes instruction and secondary school classroom teachers, 1250 minutes instruction in each period of five instructional days.

A board can allocate to each school a share of the board's aggregate minimum time for a school year for all of its classroom teachers and the principal of a school must then allocate the school's share of the board's aggregate minimum time among its classroom teachers as the principal sees fit.

POWERS OF BOARDS

A board's powers, as distinct from its duties, cover employees, courses of study and supplies, property, extra-curricular activities, expenses and agreements.[12] Boards have the power to appoint officers, teachers and staff, supervisors of teaching staff, psychiatrists, psychologists and guidance counselors, and can allow principals to assign approved duties to unpaid volunteers.

Boards may provide instruction in courses of study that are prescribed or approved by the Minister, developed from curriculum guidelines issued by the Minister[13] or approved by the board where the Minister permits the board to approve courses of study.

---

[10] *Class Size*, O. Reg. 118/98.

[11] Section 170.2.

[12] See, generally, *Education* Act, s. 170.

[13] On March 2, 1999, the Ministry of Education and Training released policy documents related to the new secondary school curriculum: *Ontario Secondary Schools, Grades 9 to 12: Program and Diploma Requirements, 1999*; *Choices into Action: Guidance and Career Education Program Policy for Ontario Elementary and Secondary Schools, 1999*; and *The Ontario Curriculum, Grades 9 and 10: Program Planning and Assessment, 1999*. In the academic year 1999-2000, the government plans to implement the new curriculum for Grade 9, a provincial report card for Grade 9, a teacher-advisor system for Grades 7 to 9, the annual education plan for

As noted earlier, a board's obligation is to "provide instruction". The board has discretion in the selection and provision of the courses, provided they have Ministry sanction.

In fulfillment of its obligation to provide "adequate accommodation" for pupils, a board determines the number and kind of schools to be established and maintained[14] and the attendance area for each school, and can close schools in accordance with policies established by the board under guidelines issued by the Minister.

A board also has discretion on the provision of school libraries and resource centres, gymnasiums, cafeterias, continuing education,[15] evening classes, courses for teachers, junior kindergarten, child care facilities and day nurseries, a cadet corps, athletics, school games, field trips, free public lectures and the support of school fairs.

With respect to its property, a board can permit its school buildings, premises and buses to be used for any educational or other lawful purpose and may operate the school ground as a park, playground and/or rink during the school year, during vacation periods, or both.

A board has discretion to pay the travelling expenses and membership fees of any member of the board or teacher or officer of the board incurred in attending meetings of an educational association. The board can also make grants and pay membership fees to any such organizations.

A board may pay the costs incurred by any member of the board or by any teacher, officer or other employee of the board in successfully defending any legal proceeding brought against him or her for defamatory statements relating to the employment, suspension or dismissal of any person by the board made or published at a meeting of the board or of a committee, or for assault in disciplinary action taken in the course of duty.

AGREEMENTS BY BOARDS

Boards have the power to enter into a number of kinds of agreements.[16] Agreements may be made with: other boards; municipalities; the federal government, native bands, councils or education authorities; and colleges of applied arts and technology. They may be made for joint use of facilities with

---

Grades 7 to 9, new Ontario Student Transcripts for Grades 9 to OAC, community involvement for Grade 9, Grade 10 course profiles, and assessment and evaluation exemplars for Grade 9 courses. They also plan to release the new curriculum for Grades 11 and 12.

[14] Within the limits imposed by the new capital funding model: see discussion in Chapter 12, "Capital Funding".

[15] As defined and governed by *Continuing Education*, R.R.O. 1990, Reg. 285 (as amended to O. Reg. 97/96).

[16] *Education Act*, ss. 181-189.

other public institutions, natural science and conservation programs and transportation of pupils.

Agreements with Other Boards

A board can enter into an agreement with another board to provide the other board with:

(a) accommodation and equipment for administrative purposes;

(b) accommodation and equipment for instructional purposes;

(c) the services of teachers and other personnel; or

(d) the transportation of pupils,

that the board is authorized or required by the Act to provide for its own pupils.

If the agreement requires the construction of a school building or an addition, alteration or improvement to a school building, the agreement must provide for the payment of the cost thereof. If the other board is not required by the agreement to pay the cost of the additional accommodation, it is a permanent improvement for that board. The agreement can provide for payment of fees for pupils covered by the agreement.

A board can also enter into an agreement with another board to provide education for pupils in a school or schools operated by the other board. In that case, the board requesting the instruction must pay to the board providing the instruction the fees, if any, payable for the purpose under the regulations.

A board can also enter into an agreement with a person other than a board for accommodation for pupils on a school site that is not to be occupied or used exclusively by the board. However, the board must obtain the prior approval of the Minister to enter into negotiations with the person and an agreement can be entered into only after the proposed agreement, the plans of the school and the building of which it may be a part, and the site have been approved by the Minister.

There is also provision in the Act for agreements for transfers of a school to another board. This applies only to transfers by a French-language public board to a coterminous French-language separate board of secondary schools.

Agreements with Municipalities

One or more boards and the council of a municipality or two or more municipalities can enter into agreements for the use of existing facilities owned by one of the parties or to establish and provide for the maintenance and operation of facilities on the property of any of the parties to such agreement for cultural, recreational, athletic, educational, administrative or other community purposes. These agreements must provide for:

(a) the acquisition of any land required for the purposes of the agreement, and the manner of approving and the method of apportioning the cost thereof;

(b) the manner of approving and the method of apportioning the cost of the construction, maintenance and operation of the facilities;

(c) the details of how and when each party shall pay its portion of these costs;

(d) the regulation, control and use of the facilities including the charging of fees for admission; and

(e) the term of the agreement and how it can be terminated.

If the subject property of the agreement is a "community recreation centre", it can be considered by the Minister of Community and Social Services as a community recreation centre for the purposes of making grants under the *Community Recreation Centres Act.*[17]

If any of these agreements require a "permanent improvement",[18] the Minister must approve the plans and specifications required by him or her before the agreement can be implemented.

Agreements with Federal Government

There are agreements which a board may enter into with the federal government or with a band, band council or education authority with respect to Indian pupils.[19]

An agreement with the federal government can provide for education by the board of pupils who reside on land held by the federal government in a school or schools operated by the board on land owned by the board or held by the federal government.[20]

There can also be agreements with the federal government providing for the federal government to pay a board to provide additional classroom accommodation, and to pay tuition for a maximum of 35 Indian pupils for each additional classroom so provided. The fees are calculated in accordance with the regulations but exclusive of expenditures for the erection of school buildings for instructional purposes and additions to the buildings.[21]

---

[17] R.S.O. 1990, c. C.22.

[18] Defined in s. 1 of the *Education Act.*

[19] "Indian", because under s. 91(24) of the *Constitution Act, 1867,* jurisdiction was conferred on the Parliament of Canada with respect to "Indians, and Lands reserved for the Indians". "Indian" is used in the Ontario *Education Act* when referring to "Indians", as defined in the *Indian Act,* R.S.C. 1985, c. I-5 (as amended to 1996, c. 23), and "Indian pupils" and "Indian schools" under the jurisdiction of federal legislation. Elsewhere in the Act, "native" is used, as in "native representation on boards".

[20] *Education Act,* s. 187.

[21] Section 188(3).

Agreements can be entered into with either the federal government or with a band, band council or education authority[22] which is authorized by the government to provide education for Indians. There are two kinds of these agreements.

The first kind of agreement is an agreement to provide accommodation, instruction and special services in the schools of the board. The agreement must provide for the payment by the government, the band, the council or the education authority of fees calculated in accordance with the regulation governing the fees payable by Canada.[23]

The second kind of agreement is an agreement for the board to provide for Indian pupils instruction and special services in schools provided by the government to the band, council or education authority. These agreements must provide for payment of the full cost of the provision of the instruction and special services.[24]

The board of an elementary school can allow any of its pupils to attend a school for Indian children of a band, council or education authority which is authorized by the federal government to provide education for Indians.[25]

The Act as amended by Bill 160 authorizes Cabinet to make regulations "providing for representation on boards, by appointment, of the interests of members of bands in respect of which there is agreement under this Act to provide instruction to pupils who are Indians within the meaning of the *Indian Act* (Canada)".[26] The representation of natives on boards is an area in which Bill 160 has transferred power from the legislature to Cabinet.

Before Bill 160, the *Education Act* provided for the appointment by a board of a person named by a council of a band to represent the interests of Indian pupils. The power of appointment arose where there was an agreement between a board and the federal government or a band council to provide for Indian pupils.

The regulations may now provide for the type and extent of participation by the persons appointed and that appointees be deemed to be elected members of the board for all purposes or for such purposes as are specified in the regulation. An appointee on a Roman Catholic board must be a Roman Catholic and at least 18 years of age; an appointee on a French-language district school board, a French-language rights holder and at least 18 years of age.

Cabinet has exercised its regulation-making power. The provisions of the regulation are virtually identical to the provisions which were formerly in the

---

[22] An "education authority" is defined in s. 1(1) of the *Education Act* as "a corporation that is incorporated by one or more bands or councils of bands for the purpose of providing for the educational needs of the members of the band or bands".

[23] Section 188(1).

[24] Section 188(2).

[25] Section 185.

[26] Section 188(5). See *Native Representation on Boards*, O. Reg. 462/97.

Act. Now, however, the regulation can be amended or revoked without recourse to the legislature.

Agreements with Community Colleges and Groups

With the approval of the Minister, a board can "in respect of persons who reside in the area of jurisdiction of the board, enter into an agreement in writing with a college of applied arts and technology for the area in which the board has jurisdiction under which the college of applied arts and technology provides for the board such adult basic education as is specified in the agreement".[27] A board can also enter into an agreement in writing with a community group for the provision by the group of Ministry-approved adult basic education for residents within the board's jurisdiction.[28] "Adult basic education" means programs and courses to develop and improve the basic literacy and numeracy skills of adults.[29]

Joint Use Agreements with Other Public Institutions

These agreements are authorized by amendments to the Act made in 1996.[30] A board can enter into an agreement with another board or with a municipality, hospital, university or college for one or more of the following purposes:

   (i)   the joint provision or use of transportation services;
  (ii)   the joint provision or use of administrative or operational support services;
 (iii)   the joint provision or use of support services for educational programs;
 (iv)   the joint provision or use of equipment or facilities of administration for operational purposes;
  (v)   the joint investment of funds; and
 (vi)   purposes prescribed by regulation.[31]

The organization with which a board may contract for joint use and the joint uses themselves may be extended by regulation but no regulation has yet been made.

---

[27] Section 189(2).
[28] Section 189(3).
[29] Section 189(1).
[30] 1996, c. 13.
[31] Section 171.1(2).

Agreements for Natural Science and Conservation Programs[32]

Two or more boards may enter into an agreement for the shared use of a school site in Ontario for conducting natural science programs and other out-of-classroom programs. If under the agreement a board may purchase or lease a school site or is to erect, add to or alter a building or make other improvements to a site, the agreement must be approved by the Minister. A school site out of the jurisdiction of the boards that are parties to the agreement cannot be acquired without the approval of the Minister.

A board may enter into an agreement with a conservation or other appropriate authority under which the board may, with the approval of the Minister, construct and maintain on lands owned by the authority facilities for a natural science program or other out-of-classroom program. A board that conducts a natural science, conservation or other out-of-classroom program may enter into an agreement with a conservation or other appropriate authority for the use of the facilities and personnel of the authority for the purpose of conducting the program. One or more boards may enter into an agreement with a conservation or other appropriate authority to provide for the construction, furnishing and equipping by the authority on lands owned by the authority of facilities for the purposes of conducting a natural science, observation or other out-of-classroom program as directed by the board or one or more of the boards. If the board is to pay all or part of the cost of the facilities, the construction of the facilities must first be approved by the Minister. The amount paid by the board is deemed to be an expenditure made by the board for a permanent improvement.

A board can provide or pay for board and lodging for a pupil for up to two weeks in a year while the pupil participates, with the consent of his or her parent or guardian and with the permission of the board, in a natural science, conservation or other out-of-classroom program.

Agreements for Transportation of Pupils[33]

A board can enter an agreement with another board for the transportation of resident pupils of the other board. In addition to its own pupils, a board can also provide transportation for pupils for whom the Ministry pays, for pupils in a hearing-handicapped program and for persons who are qualified to be resident pupils of the board to and from the Ontario School for the Blind, an Ontario school for the deaf, demonstration schools and facilities for specified health treatment, and centres operated by an affiliate of the Ontario Association for Community Living.[34]

---

[32] Section 197(5)-(9).
[33] Section 190.
[34] Section 190(3), (4).

For all these purposes, the board can make agreements for up to one year with carriers and up to five years, with Ontario Municipal Board approval, for the transportation of more than 30 pupils.[35] Boards may also buy vehicles for authorized transportation purposes, either from current revenue or from a debenture issued for the purpose.

SPECIAL EDUCATION

Special education[36] is a specific statutory obligation of the Minister but the Minister may, with Cabinet approval, make regulations with respect to special education programs and services, and identification, placement and review committees. Cabinet can make regulations governing special education advisory committees.[37]

The Act requires every district school board to establish a special education advisory committee[38] and the regulations impose significant obligations on boards with respect to these committees and the maintenance of special education plans.[39]

Every board must maintain a special education plan and ensure that the plan is amended from time to time to meet the current needs of the exceptional pupils of the board. The special education plan of the board must be reviewed annually by the board; the review must be completed prior to May 15 each year.

The special education plan of the board must provide for the enrolment and placement of each trainable retarded child who is in attendance at a day nursery licensed under the *Day Nurseries Act*[40] that has a program for developmentally handicapped children, and is qualified to be a resident pupil of the board. It must provide for the enrolment and placement of each person under the age of 21 who is qualified to be a resident pupil of the board and who resides or is lodged within the area of jurisdiction of the board in a centre, facility, home,

---

[35] Section 190(6), (7).

[36] Special education is provided for exceptional pupils. An "exceptional pupil" is defined in s. 1(1) of the Act as "a pupil whose behavioural, communicational, intellectual, physical or multiple exceptionalities are such that he or she is considered to need placement in a special education program".

[37] Section 11(1), para. 5.

[38] Section 57.1(1).

[39] Special education plans are governed by *Special Education Programs and Services*, R.R.O. 1990, Reg. 306. Advisory committees are governed by *Special Education Advisory Committees*, O. Reg. 464/97. The regulation, *Special Education Identification Placement and Review Committees and Appeals*, R.R.O. 1990, Reg. 305 (as amended to O. Reg. 663/91), was revoked and replaced by O. Reg. 181/98, *Identification and Placement of Exceptional Pupils*.

[40] R.S.O. 1990, c. D.2 (as amended to 1997, c. 30).

hospital or institution, other than a private school, that is approved, designated, established, licensed or registered under any Act and in which no education program is provided by the Ministry of Education and Training or the Ministry of the Solicitor General and Correctional Services.

Each district school board must establish a special education advisory committee consisting of a representative from each local association within the area of jurisdiction of the board (to a maximum of 12), a member of the board, and representatives of Indian pupils (where applicable), with discretion to add other members who are not representatives or board members. The role of the advisory committee is to make recommendations to the board in respect of any matter affecting the establishment, development and delivery of special education programs and services for exceptional pupils of the board.

Before making a decision on a recommendation of the committee, the board must provide an opportunity for the committee to be heard before the board and any other committee of the board to which the recommendation is referred.

The board has several obligations to its advisory committee. It is obligated to provide personnel and facilities as it considers necessary for the proper functioning of the committee, including the personnel and facilities necessary to permit the use of electronic means for the holding of meetings of the committee. Within a reasonable time after the advisory committee is appointed, the board shall provide the members of the committee and their alternates with information and orientation respecting the role of the committee and of the board in relation to special education and Ministry and board policies relating to special education. It is to provide the advisory committee with the opportunity to participate in the board's annual review of its special education plan and ensure that the committee has the opportunity to participate in the board's annual budget process and to review the financial statements of the board as the statements relate to special education.

In addition to maintaining a special education plan and establishing a special education advisory committee, school boards have a third duty with respect to special education in the identification and placement of pupils[41] and reviews and appeals of any decisions dealing with such concerns. Every board is obliged to:

(a) establish one or more committees for the identification and placement of exceptional pupils;

(b) determine the jurisdiction of each committee;

(c) establish the manner of selecting the chair of each committee; and

(d) appoint three or more persons to each committee, one of whom must be a principal employed by the board, a supervisory officer employed by the board or a person whose services are used by the board.

---

[41] See now O. Reg. 181/98, *Identification and Placement of Exceptional Pupils.*

The board must also prepare a guide for the use and information of parents and pupils containing specified provisions of the law relating to exceptional appeals and ensure the availability of the guide. Appeals from decisions of the committees are heard by a special education appeal board composed of:

(a) one member selected by the board in which the pupil is placed;

(b) one member selected by a parent of the pupil; and

(c) a chair selected jointly by the two members or where the members cannot agree by the appropriate district manager of the Ministry.

The final level of appeal is a special education tribunal.[42] The provisions with respect to special education tribunals were revised by Bill 160 and the regulation establishing special education appeal boards has been revoked.[43]

A special education tribunal is established by Cabinet to hear appeals by a parent or guardian of a pupil who has exhausted all rights of appeal under the regulations in respect of the identification or placement of the pupil as an exceptional pupil and is dissatisfied with the decision in respect of the identification or placement. The decision of the tribunal is final and binding on the parties to the decision.

SUPERVISED ALTERNATIVE LEARNING PROGRAMS

All boards are obliged to establish a supervised alternative learning for excused pupils committee.[44] The committee consists of not fewer than three persons appointed by a board. A quorum of the committee consists of:

(a) a member of the board;

(b) a supervisory officer who qualified as such as a teacher and is employed by the board, or the appropriate provincial supervisory officer; and

(c) at least one person who is not an employee of the board.

The committee considers applications for enrolment of pupils in a supervised alternative learning program as it may approve. Programs may include one or more of:

(a) full-time or part-time employment at an approved work station for a fixed term;

---

[42] *Education Act*, s. 57.

[43] Formerly R.R.O. 1990, Reg. 305 (revoked O. Reg. 181/98). See footnote 39, *supra*.

[44] Governed by *Supervised Alternative Learning for Excused Pupils*, R.R.O. 1990, Reg. 308.

(b) completion of a life skills course; and

(c) such continuing studies or other activities directed towards the pupil's needs and interests as the committee finds acceptable.

A pupil accepted into a program is excused from attendance at school either full time or part time. Regular contact with the pupil is maintained by a teacher or other staff member of the school where the pupil is enrolled to ensure that the pupil continues to conform to the program.

If a parent disagrees with a decision of the committee, he or she can notify the provincial school attendance counselor of the disagreement and the reasons for disagreeing. The provincial school attendance counselor may inquire into the validity of the parent's request to have a program prescribed for the child and recommend that the child attend school or may recommend, if satisfied that the child should be excused from attendance at school, that a program be prescribed for the pupil and send back the application to the committee for reconsideration. A committee to whom an application is sent back must reconsider the application but the committee has the final decision.

6

Organization of Boards

BOARD MEETINGS

A "board" within the meaning of the Act and other applicable law is "constituted", that is becomes a legal entity, when a majority of the members to be elected or appointed has been elected or appointed.[1]

Inaugural Meeting

A board must hold its first meeting within a week after the day on which the term of office of the board commences or, failing that, at 8 p.m. at the head office of the board on the first Wednesday following the beginning of the term of office.[2] On the petition of a majority of the members of a newly elected or appointed board, however, a supervisory officer may provide for calling the first meeting of the board at some other time and date.[3]

Annual Meetings[4]

At the first meeting in December of each year, the director of education presides until the election of the chair. At that meeting, or if a vacancy occurs in the office of chair, at the first meeting thereafter, the members elect one of themselves to be chair and the chair presides at all meetings. The members of the board may also elect one of themselves to be the vice-chair and he or she shall preside in the absence of the chair. If there is an equality of votes at the election of a chair or vice-chair, the candidates draw lots to fill the position.

The member presiding at a meeting may vote with the other members of the board on all motions. Any motion on which there is an equality of votes is lost.

A quorum consists of a majority of the members.

---

[1] *Education Act*, s. 208(1).
[2] Section 208(2).
[3] Section 208(3).
[4] Section 208(4), (5), (7), (8), (11), (12).

Chair and Vice-Chair

The Act establishes the process for the election of the chair and vice-chair but says little of their role or function. The only specific powers given to the chair are to call special meetings of the board, to preside at meetings, to vote with the other trustees on all motions and to expel or exclude from a meeting any person (including a trustee or member of the public) for "improper conduct" at a meeting.[5]

The Act does not define "improper conduct" but it is confined to conduct at the particular meeting. A guide as to what would be included in "improper conduct" is s. 212 of the Act which makes it an offence to disrupt or endeavour to disturb or interrupt a meeting after having been expelled or excluded from the meeting, with intent to prevent the discussion of any matter or the passing of any motion at the meeting. This applies to meetings of the board or a committee of a board, including a committee of the whole board.

The position of chair is not an easy one. He or she must balance the role of leader with the obligation to follow the direction of the board and ensure that its decisions are implemented. In most boards, the chair participates in setting the agenda for meetings with the director with input from other trustees and senior administrative staff. The chair works closely with the administration to ensure that the board's wishes are understood and with the board to convey information and recommendations of the administration.

Ultimately, it is the chair's obligation to ensure that meetings of the board are orderly and productive, that the trustees are fully informed, that debate is open and that conflicts are temperately resolved.

Public Access to Meetings[6]

Meetings of boards and committees of boards, including a committee of the whole board, must be open to the public. No one can be excluded from a meeting that is open to the public, except for improper conduct.

Certain matters, however, may be considered by a committee, including a committee of the whole board, in private session. These matters include:

(a) security of board property;
(b) disclosure of intimate, personal or financial information in respect of a member of the board or committee, an employee or prospective employee of the board, a pupil or his or her parent or guardian;
(c) acquisition or disposal of a school site;
(d) decisions in respect of negotiations with board employees; and
(e) litigation affecting the board.

---

[5] Section 207(3). See also s. 212(2).
[6] Section 207.

Most boards have policies governing private sessions. Generally, only board members, administrative staff such as the board secretary, and anyone directly involved with the issue are permitted to be present. Members of the public, the media and others must leave the boardroom until the private session ends.

Discussions in private session are confidential. They are not recorded in the minutes and may not be disclosed to anyone not present at the meeting. Every resolution passed in private must be adopted formally in public session.

The public records of a board are open to the public. These records are the minute book, the audited annual financial reports and the current accounts of the board.

These records may be inspected at all reasonable hours at the head office of the board. Upon written request of any person and payment to the board at the rate of 25 cents for every 100 words or at a lower rate fixed by the board, the secretary must furnish copies or extracts of the requested documents certified under the secretary's hand. In all other respects, access to documents of a board is governed by the *Municipal Freedom of Information and Protection of Privacy Act.*[7]

Electronic Meetings

A welcome innovation introduced by Bill 160 is the provision enabling the holding of meetings of the board and its committees by electronic means. Under the *Education Act*, Cabinet is given the power to make regulations for the use of electronic means for the holding of meetings of boards and board committees.[8]

Under the regulation currently in force,[9] every district school board must develop and implement a policy providing for the use of electronic means for the holding of meetings of a district school board and meetings of committees of a district school board, including a committee of the whole board. The board policy must be in accordance with the regulation and with any policies established or guidelines issued by the Minister.

There are a number of mandatory provisions with which the board's policy must comply. If a member or pupil representative so requests, the board must

---

[7] R.S.O. 1990, c. M.56 (as amended to 1997, c. 25). However, the Education Quality and Accountability Office (see discussion of office in Chapter 3, "Provincial Agencies") may require a board under s. 4 of the *Education Quality and Accountability Office Act,* 1996, S.O. 1996, c. 11 (as amended to 1997, c. 31), to provide information to it which is "personal information" within the meaning of s. 38 of the *Freedom of Information and Protection of Privacy Act,* R.S.O. 1990, c. F.31 (as amended to 1998, c. 26).

[8] Section 208.1(1)).

[9] *Electronic Meetings,* O. Reg. 463/97.

provide him or her with electronic means for participating in board meetings. The electronic means must permit the member or representative to hear and be heard by all other participants in the meeting. The electronic means must be provided to ensure that the rules governing conflict of interest of members are complied with. The policy must enable the board to refuse to provide a member with electronic means of participation in a meeting where to do so is necessary to ensure compliance with the regulation. The board's policy must also provide for participation by pupil representatives and members of the public through electronic means, except in the case of meetings closed to the public.

Every board must determine, in accordance with any policies and guidelines issued by the Minister, whether electronic means should be provided at one or more locations within its area of jurisdiction to permit participation of the public in meetings. The board's policy must provide for the extent and manner of participation by members of the public through electronic means. The policy must also ensure that members of the public who are participating through electronic means do not participate in any proceedings that are closed to the public.

The board policy must require that, at every meeting of the board or of a committee of the whole board, the following persons be physically present in the meeting room of the board:

(a) the chair of the board or his or her designate;
(b) at least one additional member of the board; and
(c) the director of education of the board or his or her designate.

In the case of other board committees, there need be no member present except the chair or designate.

Except in the case of meetings in private session, the meeting room of the board or of a committee of the board must be open to allow physical attendance by members of the public at every meeting of the board or committee of the board.

Despite these provisions, every member of a board must be physically present in the meeting room of the board for at least three regular meetings of the board in each 12-month period beginning December 1. In addition, every member must be physically present in the meeting room of the board for at least one regular meeting of the board for each period of four full calendar months following election or appointment and ending on the following November 30.

BOARD COMMITTEES

A board may but is not obliged to establish the following committees:

(a) committees of trustees to make recommendations to the board in respect of education, finance, personnel and property;[10]
(b) committees which may include persons who are not members of the board in respect of any other matters;[11]
(c) a school board advisory committee.[12]

The school board advisory committee is the only committee specifically described in the Act. If established, it must be composed of:

(a) three members of the board appointed by the board;
(b) the chief education officer of the board or his or her nominee;
(c) six teachers employed by the board and appointed by the teachers in the employ of the board;
(d) four persons appointed by the board who are neither teachers nor members of a board but who are resident within the jurisdiction of the board; and
(e) persons specific to each of the four types of school boards.

An English-language public district school board must appoint to the committee two persons selected by the home and school council if the council so recommends. A French-language public district school board must appoint to the committee one person selected by the regional section of the Fédération des associations de parents francophones de l'Ontario and, where there is no regional section, by the local section of the fédération.

An English-language separate district school board must appoint to the committee two persons selected by the diocesan council or councils of the Federation of Catholic Parent-Teacher Associations of Ontario if the council so recommends. A French-language separate district school board must appoint to the committee two Roman Catholics selected by the regional section of the Fédération des associations de parents francophones de l'Ontario.

The committee may make reports and recommendations to the board in respect of any educational matter relating to the schools under the jurisdiction of the board with the exception of the salaries of employees of the board and personnel problems and policies.

---

[10] Section 171(1), para. 1.
[11] Section 171(1), para. 2.
[12] Sections 200 to 205.

The board must consider any report or recommendation submitted to it by the committee and cannot refuse its approval without having given the committee or its representatives an opportunity to be heard by the board.

Other committees of a board are either standing (permanent) committees or ad hoc committees set up to consider and report on a specific issue.

Standing committees deal with matters of an ongoing nature such as those specified in the legislation; they are usually authorized in the board's by-laws. A standing committee is comprised of trustees. Members of staff are usually assigned to the committee to provide expertise, information and administrative support but only trustees can vote.

PUPIL REPRESENTATION ON BOARDS

The representation of pupils on boards was introduced by Bill 160 and is governed by regulation made in accordance with the Act.[13] The Act provides that a pupil representative is not a member of the board, can have no voting rights and cannot be present at any meeting in private session.

Under the regulation, every board must develop and implement a policy providing for the representation of the interests of pupils on the board. The policy must comply with the regulation and with any policies and guidelines issued by the Minister.

Each board must have at least one pupil representative who must be in the last two years of the intermediate division or in the senior division at the time that he or she is elected or appointed.

The policy must specify whether the pupil representatives are to be chosen by peer election or appointment and the procedures for choosing the representatives. The procedures must ensure that the elections or appointments be not later than June 30 in each school year, to take effect in the following school year.

The policy must specify the type and extent of participation by pupil representatives,[14] their term of office, disqualifications and the procedure for filling of vacancies. The policy must provide that pupil representatives have at least the same opportunity for participation at meetings of the board and meetings of committees of the board as a board member has.[15]

The policy may provide for reimbursement of pupil representatives for their out-of-pocket expenses reasonably incurred in connection with carrying out their responsibilities.

---

[13] *Education Act*, s. 55; O. Reg. 463/97.
[14] Subject to restrictions in the Act: see s. 55.
[15] Subject to restrictions in the Act.

7

Members of Boards

QUALIFICATIONS AND VOTING

A person is qualified[1] to be elected as a member of a district school board[2]or school authority if the person is qualified to vote for members of that district school board or school authority and is resident in its area of jurisdiction. Only those qualified to vote for a board may be a member of that board.

A person is entitled to vote in an area of jurisdiction of a board if (a) he or she at any time during the qualification period resides in the area or is an owner or tenant of residential property in the area or is a spouse of that person, and (b) on voting day:

  (i) is a Canadian citizen;
  (ii) is at least 18 years old; and
  (iii) is not a person not specifically prohibited from voting by the *Municipal Elections Act, 1996.*[3]

The members of a French-language public district school board are elected by persons entitled to vote in the area of jurisdiction of the board who are qualified to be electors for a French-language district school board and are not separate school supporters or persons entered on a preliminary list. The members of a French-language separate district school board are elected by persons entitled to vote in the area of jurisdiction of the board who are qualified to be electors for a French-language district school board and are separate school supporters or persons entered on a preliminary list.

The persons qualified to be electors for a French-language district school board are persons entitled to vote in the area of jurisdiction of the board who

---

[1] See, generally, Part VII of the Act, "Board Members — Qualifications, Resignations and Vacancies".
[2] The term "trustee" was replaced by "member of a board" by Bill 104 but the Act allows a member of a board to be referred to as a trustee for all purposes of the Act.
[3] S.O. 1996, c. 32, s. 1(1)(Sch.) (as amended to 1997, c. 31), s. 17(3).

(a) are French-language district school board supporters, and (b) are entered on a preliminary list in respect of a French-language separate or public district school board. A person qualified to be an elector for a French-language district school board cannot vote for members of an English-language district school board.

The members of an English-language separate district school board are elected by persons entitled to vote in the area of jurisdiction of the board who (a) are not qualified to be electors for a French-language district school board, and (b) are separate school supporters or persons entered on a preliminary list. The members of an English-language public district school board are elected by persons entitled to vote in the area of jurisdiction of the board who (a) are not qualified to be electors for a French-language district school board, and (b) are not separate school supporters or persons entered on a preliminary list.

An English-speaking Roman Catholic may vote for either an English-language separate school board (by choosing to be a separate school supporter) or an English-language public board. An English-speaking Roman Catholic who chooses to be a separate school supporter cannot be a member of a public school board. An English-speaking person who is not a Roman Catholic may vote only for and be a member only of an English-language public school board.

A French-speaking Roman Catholic may vote for either a French-language separate school board (by choosing to be a separate school supporter) or a French-language public board. A French-speaking Roman Catholic who chooses to be a separate school supporter cannot be a member of a public school board. A French-speaking person may vote only for and be a member only of a French-language board. A Roman Catholic, English-speaking or French-speaking, who chooses not to be a separate school supporter may be a member of a public school board, English or French, as the case requires.

Thus, those who are defined by denomination (Roman Catholic) have a choice whether or not to vote for the board of their denomination. Those who are defined by their language, French or English, have no choice whether or not to vote for the board of their language. Similarly, an English-speaking non-Roman Catholic has no choice. He or she can vote only for an English-language public board.

Roman Catholics, French and English, are the only "class of persons" who have a choice, a choice which is protected by s. 93(1) of the *Constitution Act, 1867*.[4]

All the qualifications and restrictions which apply to the right to vote for a member of a board also determine the right to be a member of the board.

---

[4] See Chapter 1 under heading "Constitutional Protections".

DISQUALIFICATIONS[5]

The following are prohibited from voting and are therefore disqualified from being a trustee:

(i) a person who is serving a sentence of imprisonment in a penal or correctional institution;

(ii) a corporation;

(iii) a person acting as an executor, a trustee or in any other representative capacity except as a voting proxy; and

(iv) a person who was convicted of a corrupt practice (for four years after he or she was convicted).[6]

The Act also provides that a person is disqualified from being elected as a member of a school board or school authority if he or she is:

(a) an employee or the spouse of any district school board or school authority (unless he or she takes an unpaid leave of absence beginning no later than nomination day and ending on voting day);

(b) the clerk, treasurer, deputy clerk or deputy treasurer of a county or municipality, any part of which is included in the area of jurisdiction of the district school board or the school authority;

(c) a member of the Legislative Assembly, the Senate or the House of Commons of Canada; or

(d) a person who is otherwise ineligible or disqualified under this or any other Act.

The disqualification of spouses of employees of boards or school authorities was the subject of a court challenge on the ground that it discriminated against a group on the basis of their spousal or family status. The Ontario Court of Appeal upheld the challenge, thus removing this disqualification from the Act.[7]

A person is not qualified to be elected in a by-election or to act as member of a district school board if he or she is already:

(a) a member of some other district school board;

(b) a member of a school authority;

(c) a member of the council of a county or municipality or an elected member of a local board of a county or municipality, all or part of

---

[5] *Education Act*, s. 219(4).

[6] Corrupt practices are listed in s. 90(3) of the *Municipal Elections Act, 1996*.

[7] *Ontario Public School Boards' Assn. v. Ontario (Attorney General)* (1998), 151 D.L.R. (4th) 346 (Ont. Ct. (Gen. Div.)), revd on this point 89 A.C.W.S. (3d) 689 (C.A.).

which is included in the area of jurisdiction of the district school board,

and the person's term of office has at least two months to run after the last day for filing nominations for the by-election (unless the person resigns the position before the closing of nominations). A person is not qualified to be elected in a by-election or to act as a member of a school authority if the person is:

(a) a member of some other school authority;

(b) a member of a district school board;

(c) a member of the council of a county or municipality, including a regional municipality, the County of Oxford and the District Municipality of Muskoka, all or part of which is included in the area of jurisdiction of the school authority; or

(d) an elected member of a local board as defined in the *Municipal Affairs Act*,[8] a county or municipality, including a regional municipality, the County of Oxford and the District Municipality of Muskoka, all or part of which is included in the area of jurisdiction of the school authority,

and the person's term of office has at least two months to run after the last day for filing nominations for the by-election (unless the person resigns before the closing of nominations).

No one can run as a candidate for more than one seat on a school board or school authority. If a person does so and is elected to hold one or more seats on the school board or school authority, the person is not entitled to act as a member of the board or school authority by reason of the election.

A member ceases to be qualified to act as a member if the person ceases to hold the qualifications required to be elected as a member of the board or school authority.

DECLARATION AND OATH OF OFFICE

Every newly elected or appointed member of a board must make a declaration and the oath of affirmation of office, in English or French, before the secretary of the board or before a person authorized to administer an oath or affirmation. The wording of the declaration is:

---

[8] R.S.O. 1990, c. M.46 (as amended to 1993, c. 27).

I, _____, do solemnly swear that:

1. I am not disqualified under any Act from being a member of (*name of board*).
2. I will truly, faithfully, impartially and to the best of my ability execute the office of board member, and that I have not received and will not receive any payment or reward or promise thereof for the exercise of any partiality or malversation or other undue execution of the said office and that I will disclose any pecuniary interest, direct or indirect, as required by and in accordance with the *Municipal Conflict of Interest Act*.

Declared before me at
_____ in the Province of Ontario
_____ this _____ day of _____, 19 .

The oath of affirmation of officers is:

I, _____, do (swear or affirm) that I will be faithful and bear true allegiance to Her Majesty, Queen Elizabeth II (or the reigning sovereign for the time being).

(Sworn or affirmed) before me at
_____ in the Province of Ontario
_____ this _____ day of _____,19 .

The declaration must be made on or before the day of the first meeting of the board after the member's election or appointment or on or before the day of the first meeting the person attends. The oath or affirmation of allegiance must be taken before the member enters on his or her duties as a member. If a member fails to make the declaration, he or she is considered to have resigned. A member who fails to take the oath or affirmation of allegiance remains a member of the board but cannot enter on his or her duties as a member.

HONORARIA[9]

Before Bill 160, trustees received allowances, the amount of which was determined by each board. There was no limit on the amount of the allowances. Trustees now, however, receive honoraria. The amount is still determined by each board but it cannot exceed $5,000 per year. An additional honorarium

---

[9] See, generally, *Education* Act, ss. 191-191.2.

may be paid to the chair and vice-chair but it cannot exceed the amount of the honoraria paid to the trustees. A board can also provide for a deduction of a reasonable amount from honoraria because of absence of a member from meetings of the board or a board committee.

The provisions governing travel expenses remain the same as before but in addition a board may now establish a policy under which a member may be reimbursed for all or part of any out-of-pocket expenses reasonably incurred "in connection with carrying out the responsibilities of a board member".

A school authority may pay to its members an honorarium and to its chair and vice-chair an additional honorarium at the same rate and on the same conditions as the allowance being paid to its members on December 1, 1996.

Cabinet may make regulations governing the payment of honoraria to members of a school authority, including its chair and vice-chair. No regulations have been made as yet.

CONFLICTS OF INTEREST

Conflicts of interest of trustees are governed by the *Municipal Conflict of Interest Act*,[10] originally passed in 1983. Its intended replacement, the *Local Government Disclosure of Interest Act, 1994*[11] was passed in 1994 but has never been proclaimed in force.

The "interests" provided for in the 1983 Act are strictly "pecuniary". There are three kinds of pecuniary interest referred to in the Act: "direct"; "indirect"; and "deemed". The only one which is defined is an "indirect pecuniary interest", which arises when a trustee or his or her nominee:

    (a) is a shareholder in or a director or senior officer of a private corporation;

    (b) has a controlling interest in or is a director or senior officer of a public corporation; or

    (c) is a member of a body,

that has a pecuniary interest in the matter, or when the trustee is a partner of or is employed by a person or body that has a pecuniary interest in the matter.

The only "deemed" pecuniary interest referred to in the Act is known as direct or indirect interest of a trustee's "parent", "spouse" or "child", all of which have extended definitions. There is a list of "interests" in the Act which are not "pecuniary interests" for the purposes of the Act.

---

[10] R.S.O. 1990, c. M.50 (as amended to 1997, c. 31).
[11] R.S.O. 1994, c. 23, Sch. B (as amended to 1997, c. 31).

Where a trustee has a conflict of interest, direct or indirect, in any matter and is present at a board "meeting" considering that matter, the trustee must disclose the interest and its general nature before any consideration of the matter at the meeting. The trustee cannot take part in the discussion of or vote on the matter and must not attempt to influence the voting on the question in any way before, during or after the meeting. If the meeting is not open to the public, the member must also leave the meeting or that part of the meeting during which the matter is under consideration.

If the trustee is not present at the meeting, he or she must disclose the interest at the next meeting of the board the trustee attends. The disclosure does not have to be in writing but does have to be recorded in the minutes.

A "meeting" for these purposes includes any regular, special, committee or other meeting of the board but the Act does not define "committee" so it is unclear whether it includes advisory committees and subcommittees.

If the number of members remaining after declarations of conflict of interest is less than a quorum, the remaining members are deemed to be a quorum (unless fewer than two members remain). In that event, the board can apply to a judge for an order enabling it to discuss and vote on the matter.

An application can also be made to a judge, by an elector, to determine whether there has been a breach of the Act by a trustee. If the judge finds a contravention, the judge must declare the trustee's seat vacant. The judge also has the power to disqualify the trustee from being a trustee for up to seven years and to order restitution of any financial gain to an injured party if ascertainable and, if not ascertainable, to the board. If the breach of the Act is held to be inadvertent or an error in judgment, the seat is not vacated and the trustee is not be disqualified but the restitution requirement continues to apply.

The proceedings of the board are not automatically void because a trustee has breached the Act but are voidable by court order at the instance of the board. The decision of a board will not be made void if to do so would adversely affect a third party.

The *Local Government Disclosure of Interest Act 1994*, would remedy many of the shortcomings and clarify the ambiguities of the present legislation. The 1994 Act contains additional provisions governing the acceptance by a trustee of fees, gifts and personal benefits, and requiring trustees to file annually a comprehensive disclosure statement of finances and assets. The Act would also create a position of commissioner to enforce and oversee the application of the Act.

The announced reason for withholding proclamation of the 1994 Act was that although a committee of municipal councillors, school trustees and public utility trustees had recommended "good" changes to the Act, the Association of Municipalities of Ontario had complained that the proposed law was harder on local officials than the one applying to members of the legislature. The "good changes" have yet to be made. There was also widespread concern over the extent of financial disclosure which would be required.

VACANCIES AND RESIGNATIONS[12]

The seat of a member of a school board or school authority who is not qualified or entitled to act as a member of that board or school authority is vacated. A member of a board vacates his or her seat if he or she:

(a) is convicted of an indictable offence and the time for appealing from the conviction has elapsed or any appeal has been finally determined (but if the conviction is quashed on appeal, the seat is deemed not to have been vacated);

(b) absents him or herself without being authorized by resolution in the minutes from three consecutive regular meetings of the board;

(c) ceases to hold the qualifications required to act as a member of the board;

(d) becomes disqualified;

(e) fails to be physically present in the meeting room of the board for at least three regular meetings of the board in each 12-month period beginning December 1; or

(f) for the period beginning with election or appointment to the board to fill a vacancy until the following November 30, fails to be physically present in the meeting room of the board for each period of four full calendar months during that period.

If a vacancy occurs on a board, the procedure to fill the vacancy depends on whether a majority of the elected members remain in office. If a majority remains, they must appoint a qualified person to fill the vacancy within 60 days after the office becomes vacant. However, if the vacancy occurs in a non-election year or before April 1 in the year of a regular election, the remaining elected members can by resolution require that an election be held to fill the vacancy. If a majority does not remain in office, a by-election must be held to fill the vacancy, in the same manner as an election of the board.[13]

If a vacancy occurs on a board within one month before the next election, it cannot be filled. If a vacancy occurs after the election but before the new board is organized, it must be filled immediately after the new board is organized in the same way as a vacancy that occurs after the board is organized.

---

[12] *Education Act*, ss. 220-228.

[13] By-elections held on or before March 31, 2000, are governed by O. Reg. 79/98, *By-elections.*

A member appointed or elected to fill a vacancy holds office for the remainder of the term of the member who vacated the office.

Where no qualified persons or an insufficient number of qualified persons are available or the electors have failed to elect a sufficient number of members of a board to form a quorum, the Minister can appoint members of the board. The persons so appointed have, during the term of their appointment, all the authority of board members, as though there were eligible and had been duly elected.

There are special provisions with respect to filling a vacancy on a board of less than three members, vacancies on rural separate school boards and failure or inability to fill a vacancy.

Where a member of a board has to resign to become a candidate for some other office, the member resigns by filing the resignation with the secretary of the board, with a statement that the resignation is for the purpose of becoming a candidate for some other office. The resignation becomes effective on the earlier of the November 30 after it is filed or the day before the day on which the term of the other office commences.

In any other circumstance, a member can resign only with the consent of a majority of the members present at a meeting, with the consent entered on the minutes of the meeting, and only if the resignation will not reduce the number of members of the board to less than a quorum. The member cannot vote on the motion as to his or her own resignation.

INSURANCE FOR BOARD MEMBERS

A board has the power to take out insurance to cover its members and "members of an advisory committee" appointed by the board.[14] The insurance must be by contract with an issuer licensed under the *Insurance Act*[15] and may be:

(a) group accident insurance to indemnify the insured or his or her estate against loss resulting from accident or death; and

(b) group public liability and property damage insurance to indemnify the insured or his or her estate for loss or damage for which he or she has become liable by reason of injury to persons or property or in respect of loss or damage suffered by him or her by reason of injury to his or her own property,

---

[14] *Education Act*, s. 176. The quoted wording is broad enough to include members of any committee which a board has the power to establish who are not members of the board. See discussion of committees in Chapter 6 under heading "Board Committees".

[15] R.S.O. 1990, c. I.8 (as amended to 1997, c. 43).

while travelling on the business of the board, within or outside the area of the board's jurisdiction, in performance of duties either as a member of the board or an advisory committee.

Before Bill 160, a board could also provide for its members any of the life insurance and hospital and health services benefits which it can provide for its employees. It can no longer do so.

8

Administration of Boards

The administration of school boards and schools consists of:

(i)   the director of education;
(ii) officers of the board;
(iii) supervisory officers;
(iv) other staff employees;
(v) principals;
(vi) teachers; and
(vii) school councils.

DIRECTORS OF EDUCATION[1]

School Boards

The director of education is the chief education officer and the chief executive officer of the board by which he or she is employed. Before Bill 160, a board of education or a separate school board was obliged to appoint a director of education only if the board had an enrolment of 2,000 or more students. Now, however, every district school board must employ a director of education and supervisory officers to supervise all aspects of the programs under its jurisdiction. A director of education must be a supervisory officer and a qualified teacher.

The statutory obligations of the director of education are, within policies established by the board, "to develop and maintain an effective organization and the programs to implement such policies".[2]

The director of education must submit an annual report to the board on the fulfilment of these statutory obligations. The report is submitted, in a format

---

[1] See, generally, *Education* Act, ss. 279, 280, 283.
[2] Section 283(2).

approved by the Minister, to the board at the first meeting in December, with a copy to the Minister by the following January 31.

School Authorities[3]

There are special provisions with respect to directors of education and supervisory officers for school authorities. With Ministry approval, two or more public school authorities or two or more Roman Catholic school authorities can agree to appoint a supervisory officer as director of education to supervise all aspects of the programs under their respective jurisdictions. A school authority that appoints a director of education with the approval of the Minister cannot abolish the position without the approval of the Minister.

A school authority must appoint one or more English-speaking supervisory officers for schools and classes where English is the language of instruction and one or more French-speaking supervisory officers for schools and classes where French is the language of instruction. However with Ministry approval, a school authority can enter into an agreement with another board to obtain the services of an English-speaking or French-speaking supervisory officer, appointed by the other board, or make an agreement with the Minister to obtain the services of an English-speaking or French-speaking supervisory officer appointed by the Minister.

OFFICERS OF BOARD[4]

The officers of a board are its secretary, treasurer and, if a board appoints one (or more), business administrator.

The duties of the secretary of the board are to:

(a) keep a full and correct record of the proceedings of every meeting of the board in the board's minute book and ensure that the minutes when confirmed are signed by the chair or presiding member;

(b) transmit to the Ministry copies of reports requested by the Ministry;

(c) give notice of all meetings of the board to each of the members by notifying the member personally or in writing or by sending a written notice to his or her residence;

(d) call a special meeting of the board on the request in writing of the majority of the members of the board; and

(e) perform such other duties as may be required of the secretary by the regulations, by the Act or by the board.

---

[3] See s. 284.
[4] See, generally, ss. 198, 199.

The duties of the treasurer of the board are to:

(a) receive and account for all money of the board;

(b) open an account or accounts in the name of the board in a place of deposit approved by the board;

(c) deposit all money received by the treasurer on account of the board, and no other money, to the credit of the account or accounts;

(d) disburse all money as directed by the board; and

(e) produce, when required by the board, the auditors or other competent authority, papers and money in the treasurer's possession, power or control which belong to the board.

The treasurer and, if required by the board, any other officer of a board must give security for the faithful performance of their duties. The security is to be deposited for safekeeping as directed by the board. The security must be a bond of an insurer licensed under the *Insurance Act*[5] to write surety and fidelity insurance.

If a board does not take property security from the treasurer or other person to whom it entrusts board money and any of the money is lost or forfeited, every member of the board is personally liable for the money. The money lost can be recovered by the board or by any ratepayer assessed for support of the board suing personally and on behalf of all other such ratepayers. It is a good defence in any such proceeding for the member to prove that he or she made reasonable efforts to obtain the taking of security.

If a board decides that one or more persons ought to be employed full time to carry out the duties of a secretary, treasurer or both, it can appoint one or more business administrators and assistant business administrators. The board can assign to the person appointed any of the duties of the secretary, treasurer and supervisor of maintenance of school buildings.

Every officer appointed by a board is responsible to the board through its chief executive officer for the performance of the duties assigned to him or her by the board.

The Minister has the power to establish policies and guidelines respecting the roles and responsibilities of board members, directors of education, supervisory officers, principals, superintendents and other officials.

SUPERVISORY OFFICERS[6]

A supervisory officer is defined in the Act as a person who is qualified as such in accordance with the regulations governing supervisory officers and

---

[5] R.S.O. 1990, c. I.8 (as amended to 1997, c. 43).

[6] See, generally, Part XI of the *Education Act*, "Supervisory Officers".

who is employed by a board and designated by the board or employed in the Ministry and designated by the Minister to perform such supervisory and administrative duties as are required of supervisory officers by the Act and the regulations. In general, the responsibilities of supervisory officers are defined by the Act and the qualifications necessary to become a supervisory officer are governed by regulation.[7]

When a board proposes to appoint a supervisory officer, it must notify the Minister and advise of the area of responsibility to be assigned. The appointment can be made only after the Minister has confirmed that the proposed appointee has the necessary qualifications for eligibility for the appointment. No other "approval" from the Minister is required, as is sometimes erroneously believed.

Upon the appointment being made, the board designates the title and area of responsibility of the supervisory officer and can assign to the supervisory officer administrative duties in addition to those prescribed by law. The statutory duties which a board must assign to its supervisory officer(s) are:

- assist teachers to improve the quality of education
- co-operate with boards to serve the best interests of pupils
- visit schools and prepare reports about them
- ensure that the schools are conducted in accordance with the law
- make reports to the Minister and the board as required
- report unsanitary conditions to the medical officer of health
- supervise business functions of the board
- supervise buildings and property of the board

A supervisory officer appointed by a board is responsible to the board through the chief executive officer for the performance of the duties assigned and a supervisory officer appointed by the Minister is similarly responsible to the Minister.

A supervisory officer who is responsible for the development, implementation, operation and supervision of educational programs in schools must hold a supervisory officer's certificate or be deemed to hold one as a result of the "grandfathering" provision in the regulation.

The position of a supervisory officer is a full-time one. A supervisory officer cannot hold any other office, have any other employment or follow any other profession or calling while a supervisory officer, without the Minister's approval.

The prohibitions on the paid promotion or sale of learning materials apply to supervisory officers as well as to teachers and employees of the board and the Ministry. The prohibitions are against the promotion, offers to sell and the sale directly or indirectly of any book or other teaching or learning materials, equip-

---

[7] See *Supervisory Officers*, R.R.O. 1990, Reg. 309 (as amended to O. Reg. 182/97).

ment, furniture, stationery or other article to a board, provincial school, teachers' college or pupil. Exempted from the prohibitions are books and other teaching or learning materials authored by the supervisory officer where the only compensation is a fee or royalty. Violation of the prohibitions is an offence with a fine of not more than $1,000.

BUSINESS SUPERVISORY OFFICERS[8]

Under the regulation,[9] a person can apply to and obtain from the Minister a Business Supervisory Officer's Certificate if he or she:

(i) has at least seven years of successful experience in business administration, including at least three years in a relevant managerial role;

(ii) holds an acceptable university degree;

(iii) holds a master's degree from a university or is qualified to practise as an architect, certified general accountant, certified management accountant, chartered accountant, lawyer or professional engineer, or is in another professional capacity that in the opinion of the Minister provides experience appropriate for the position of business supervisory officer;

(iv) has successfully completed a program in school board management; and

(v) has successfully completed the business supervisory officer's qualifications program within five years after starting the program.

A person who wishes to enter the qualifications program must provide to the organization or institution that provides the program proof that he or she is a qualified candidate.

The requirement of having completed a program in school board management is satisfied if the person has a Master's degree that is an acceptable university degree and has successfully completed graduate courses, as part of or in addition to the courses necessary to obtain the degree, in school board finance and school board administration. An acceptable university degree and certification as a general accountant, a certified management accountant or a chartered accountant are considered to be the equivalent of the four optional graduate courses in a program of school board management.

The business supervisory officer's qualifications program must be provided by an organization or institution that has entered into a contract with the Minis-

---

[8] The Act contains no reference to "business supervisory officers" but they are referred to by Reg. 309.

[9] See footnote 7, *supra*.

ter to run the program. The program must consist of four instructional modules, each consisting of at least 50 hours of instruction which in the opinion of the Minister are relevant to the position of business supervisory officer. The subject areas are to include:

(i) statutes, regulations and government policies affecting education in Ontario;

(ii) curriculum guidelines and other reference material pertaining to elementary and secondary education in Ontario; and

(iii) theories and practices of supervision, administration and business organization.

The program must also include one module consisting of at least 50 hours of practical experience in the workplace.

A board can appoint a person who does not hold or who under the regulation is not deemed to hold a Business Supervisory Officer's Certificate as a senior business official or as a business official for a term of not more than two years if the person:

(a) holds an acceptable university degree or is qualified to practise as an architect, certified general accountant, certified management accountant, chartered accountant, lawyer, professional engineer or in another professional capacity that in the opinion of the Minister provides appropriate experience for the position of business supervisory officer; and

(b) has entered into an agreement in writing with the board to obtain a Business Supervisory Officer's Certificate within the term of the appointment.

A board can employ the person so appointed for an additional period of not more than two years if he or she continues to make progress towards obtaining a Business Supervisory Officer's Certificate. A person so appointed and employed by a board is qualified as a business supervisory officer only for the period during which the person is employed by the board as a senior business official or business official.

A senior business official who reports to a director of education or an assistant or associate director of education is deemed to hold a Business Supervisory Officer's Certificate. A business official who:

(a) is assigned one or more of the duties of a supervisory officer;

(b) reports to a senior business official; and

(c) has been appointed to a position designated by a board as superintendent, assistant superintendent, comptroller, assistant comptroller, business administrator, assistant business administrator or an equivalent and has been approved by the Minister,

is deemed to hold a Business Supervisory Officer's Certificate. A supervisory officer who holds a Business Supervisory Officer's Certificate is qualified for business administration purposes only.

REDUNDANCY, TRANSFER, SUSPENSION AND DISMISSAL[10]

If the position held by a supervisory officer is declared by a board to be redundant, the board must:

(a) give the supervisory officer at least three months' notice in writing that the position has been declared redundant;

(b) transfer the supervisory officer to a position for which he or she is qualified with supervisory and administrative responsibilities as similar as possible to those of the previous position; and

(c) pay the supervisory officer for at least one year following the date of the transfer with no reduction in his or her rate of salary.

A redundancy occurs if the position of a supervisory officer no longer needs to be filled because of:

(a) the implementation by a board of a long-range organizational plan of operation in respect of schools or of supervisory services that eliminates the position or merges it with another position;

(b) a reduction in the number of classes or in the business functions of the board for which supervision is required; or

(c) a change in the duties or requirements placed on boards by or under any Act that renders a supervisory service unnecessary or reduces the need for such service.

Under the Act, a board can suspend or dismiss a supervisory officer in accordance with the regulations for neglect of duty, misconduct or inefficiency. Where a board does so, it must notify in writing both the supervisory officer and the Minister of the suspension or dismissal and the reasons for the dismissal. The regulation made under the Act provides that a board cannot suspend or dismiss a supervisory officer without first giving the supervisory officer reasonable information about the reasons for the suspension or dismissal and an

---

[10] Reg. 309, s. 7.

opportunity to make submissions to the board. A supervisory officer who wishes to make submissions to the board may make them orally or in writing.

PRINCIPALS

A principal of a school is a teacher appointed by a board to perform in respect of the school the duties of a principal under the Act and the applicable regulation. The main duties of principals are set out in the Act.[11] The regulation imposes duties in addition to those under the Act or assigned by the board.[12]

The listed duties of principals relate primarily to pupils, pupil records, time-tables, textbooks, examinations, health issues, supervision of instruction, performance appraisals of teachers and the making of recommendations regarding their appointment, promotion, demotion or dismissal, and reporting to the board on these matters. The role of principals in the governance structure of education is that, subject to the authority of the appropriate supervisory officer, they are in charge of the instruction and discipline of pupils in the school and the organization and management of the school.

Principals are responsible to maintain proper order and discipline in their school and "to give assiduous attention to the health and comfort of the pupils, to the cleanliness, temperature and ventilation of the school, to the care of all teaching materials and other school property, and to the condition and appearance of the school buildings and grounds".[13] They are accountable to the Ministry and to their supervisory officer to provide them with information in their power to give respecting the condition of the school premises, the discipline of the school, the progress of the pupils and any other matter affecting the interests of the school. They must provide to their board any report which the board requires.

The qualifications to become a principal and the procedure to follow to declare a principal redundant are governed by regulations.[14]

Prior to Bill 160, principals and vice-principals were obliged to be members of a branch affiliate for collective bargaining purposes and were members of a bargaining unit. Principals and vice-principals are now excluded from bargaining units which consist exclusively of teachers.[15] Following the legislative change, principals in the public system formed their own professional associa-

---

[11] Section 265.

[12] See *Operation of Schools — General*, R.R.O. 1990, Reg. 298 (as amended to O. Reg. 425/98).

[13] Section 265(j).

[14] See *Operation of Schools — General*, R.R.O. 1990, Reg. 298 (as amended to O. Reg. 425/98); *Teachers' Qualifications*, O. Reg. 184/97, made under the *Ontario College of Teachers Act, 1996*, S.O. 1996, c. 12 (as amended to 1997, c. 31); *Principals and Vice-Principals — Redundancy and Reassignment*, O. Reg. 90/98.

[15] *Education Act*, ss. 277.1-277.5.

tion, the Ontario Principals' Council. The stated objectives of the council are to:

(a) promote publicly funded education;
(b) influence educational decision-making at all levels;
(c) foster positive relations between principals, vice-principals and the broader educational community; and
(d) work with government, district school boards, school councils and other members of the educational community to ensure exemplary schools for Ontario's students.

The council provides professional services to its individual members, including legal advice and support, and to its membership generally through conferences, seminars, regular communication and links with other educational agencies. The Catholic Principals' Council of Ontario performs a similar role for principals and vice-principals in the Catholic system.

TEACHERS

In addition to their basic obligations to teach, to encourage pupils in the pursuit of learning and to inculcate by precept and example certain religious principles of moral values, teachers are required by the Act to maintain, under the direction of the principal, proper order and discipline in the classroom and while on duty in the school and on the school grounds,[16] and by regulation to:

(i) be responsible for the management of the class or classes assigned;
(ii) carry out all supervisory duties and instructional programs assigned by the principal;
(iii) assist the principal in maintaining close co-operation with the community;
(iv) ensure that all reasonable safety procedures are carried out in courses and activities for which the teacher is responsible; and
(v) co-operate with the principal and other teachers to establish and maintain consistent disciplinary practices in the school.[17]

Teachers may also be appointed by a board to direct and supervise an organizational unit of a school under the authority of the principal.[18]

There have been a number of recent changes in the law affecting teachers. Their qualifications and discipline matters are now governed by the *Ontario*

---

[16] Section 264.
[17] Reg. 298, s. 20.
[18] Reg. 298, s. 14.

College of Teachers Act, 1996.[19] A teacher must be a member of the college.[20] Boards of reference are no longer appointed in termination cases.[21] The *School Boards and Teachers Collective Negotiations Act*[22] has been repealed and replaced by Part X.1 of the *Education Act*, "Teachers' Collective Bargaining". It places collective bargaining matters for teachers under the jurisdiction of the Ontario *Labour Relations Act, 1995.*[23] Minimum times which teachers must spend in the classroom have been prescribed by statute, which override agreements reached with boards in the collective bargaining process.[24]

Despite these changes, the disruption they caused and the impact upon teacher morale which they occasioned, it will ultimately be the teachers who determine the success of the government's "student-focused" reforms.

SCHOOL COUNCILS

The only legislative provisions at present with respect to school councils, which were introduced by Bill 160, are that every board must establish a school council for each school operated by the board, in accordance with regulations made by Cabinet respecting school councils, including regulations relating to their establishment, composition and functions.[25]

Although no such regulations have yet been made,[26] the Ministry has issued a policy/program memorandum setting out the mandate of school councils and the minimum requirements for their composition and operation.[27] The minimum requirements for school councils set out in the memorandum with respect

---

[19] See now *Teachers' Qualifications*, O. Reg. 184/97, made under the *Ontario College of Teachers Act, 1996.*

[20] In s. 1(1) of the *Education Act*, "teacher" is defined as "a member of the Ontario College of Teachers".

[21] Sections 267 to 277 of the Act which provided for boards of reference were repealed by Bill 160 but they continue to apply with respect to applications for a board of reference made before September 1, 1998, and not finally determined by that date. Regulation 300 (as amended to O. Reg. 122/95), *Practice and Procedure — Boards of Reference*, as it read on August 31, 1998, also continues to apply with respect to such applications.

[22] R.S.O. 1990, c. S.2 (repealed 1997, c. 31).

[23] S.O. 1995, c. 1, Sch. A (as amended to 1998, c. 8).

[24] Section 170.2(7).

[25] Sections 17.1, 170(1), (3).

[26] The only provision in the regulations which refers to school councils requires school principals to distribute to each member of the school council materials from the Ministry identified as relevant to the functions of the school council and for distribution to the members of school councils, and to provide the names of the members of the school council to parents and, on request, to supporters of the board: Reg. 298, s. 11(12-15).

[27] *School Board Policies on School Councils*, PPM No. 122, April, 1995.

to composition and membership, elections and term of office, and roles and responsibilities have been summarized below.

Composition and Membership

- parents and guardians of students enrolled in school to form majority
- community representatives
- student representative (secondary school mandatory, elementary school at discretion of principal)
- principal
- teacher
- non-teaching staff member
- parent member elected by council to be chair
- membership to represent diversity of community
- no honorarium for council members

Elections and Term of Office

- parent representatives elected by parents and guardians of students enrolled in school
- student, teacher and non-teaching staff representatives elected by respective constituencies
- community representatives appointed by council
- principal holds designated membership
- one-year or two-year terms for elected and appointed positions
- members may seek additional terms
- at least four meetings per year.
- meetings open to all members of school community

Roles and Responsibilities

- advise principal and, where appropriate, board on any of following that council has identified as priorities:
  - local school-year calendar
  - school code of student behaviour
  - curriculum and program goals and priorities
  - responses of school and/or school board to achievement in provincial and board assessment programs
  - preparation of school profile
  - selection of principals
  - school budget priorities, including local capital-improvement plans
  - school community communication strategies
  - methods of reporting to parents and community
  - extracurricular activities in school

- school-based services and community partnerships related to social, health, recreational and nutritional programs
- community use of school facilities
- co-ordination of local services for children and youth
- development, implementation and review of board policies at local school level

In November, 1998, the Education Improvement Commission (EIC) released its report on the role of school councils which, in its own words, affirms the commission's "enthusiasm for, and the government's commitment to, parental involvement in education".[28] As the commission's report points out, the first requirement is that there be established a clear understanding of the purpose of school councils and of what they should be doing. As with every organization, the school councils' effectiveness will depend on their having a mandate which is clear and a function which has meaning. The best that the EIC has so far come up with is that "the purpose of school councils is to improve student learning, and . . . parental and community involvement is one of the means of achieving this purpose".[29] The government's stated purpose is that school councils are established "to increase the level of parental and community involvement in the education of Ontario's young people".[30]

Neither of these statements carries us very far. Is parental and community involvement a societal "good" in itself? Or is its purpose to provide some benefit to education which is not evident in the existing institutional structure? Or is it merely a "feel good" measure, intended to dissipate discontent at the local level?

No doubt the impetus for some formal vehicle for parental involvement in the schools is a feeling of powerlessness, a perception by parents that decisions are being taken which directly affect their children but over which they have neither control nor influence. The issue is how best to meet the need for some control or influence. Indeed, the first questions is: should school councils exercise control or merely influence? Put another way, are they to be decision-making entities or advisory only?

There is no discernible significant demand for decision-making authority. Such authority is equated with governance or management decisions made by principals, supervisory officers and directors of education — ordering classroom supplies, hiring and firing, negotiating contracts with employees, etc. Most parents do not wish to take on these kinds of responsibilities.

On the other hand, an advisory body is worthwhile only if it is consulted and its advice and recommendations listened to, resulting in the exercise of real

---

[28] *The Road Ahead III: A Report on the Role of School Councils* (Education Improvement Commission, November, 1998), p.1.

[29] *Ibid.*, at p. 7.

[30] *Ibid.*

influence. The recommendations of the EIC are intended to ensure that this becomes a reality.

The EIC recommends that the Ministry provide school councils with a statement of the purpose of school councils, descriptions of the roles that each representative on a school council can and in the case of the principal will play, a list of substantive topics on which councils are to be consulted and a statement of procedures that will ensure councils have time to provide input and that the input is considered. The EIC envisions that the Ministry, school boards, principals, superintendents and councils themselves each have a role in ensuring that school councils have substance.

The main recommendations of the EIC report with respect to each of these are summarized below.

Ministry, School Boards and Principals

- change their procedures to integrate school councils into policy development and implementation processes for issues within the responsibility of school councils

Ministry

- ensure that school councils are provided with support for training needs of their members
- establish code of conduct for school council members
- develop list of independent mediators approved by school board associations and Ontario Parent Council to assist school councils to resolve conflicts

School Boards

- develop process for ensuring school councils involved in development, monitoring, evaluation and reporting of board improvement plans
- establish selection criteria for principals and consult with school councils about the qualities they seek in a principal, given the specific needs of their schools
- include parent members of school councils on selection committees for principals
- as part of their evaluation policies and procedures, seek opinions of parent and community representatives on school councils on performance of principals, superintendents and directors of education
- establish in consultation with school councils a conflict resolution process for the councils in their jurisdiction

School Boards and Principals

- develop procedures to integrate school councils into school improvement planning process
- seek advice of school councils on issues identified as mandatory or which boards have determined to be priorities
- provide school councils with information about the school and board, including student achievement on provincial tests and results of other assessments of the school, students and board
- specify topics on which councils to be consulted or for which they are to have responsibility
- detail procedures councils can use to consult and communicate with all parents and community in general
- provide statement of procedures to ensure councils have time to provide input and input is considered
- provide a copy of school council handbook for each member
- detail conflict resolution strategies
- develop code of conduct
- through directors of education, publish and distribute annual report cards on performance and achievement levels of the students
- develop annual improvement plans, based on analysis of report cards that reflect academic and other expectations of board, including formal process for measuring and reporting progress toward improvement goals

Principals

- in consultation with school councils, be jointly responsible for ensuring school council membership representative of school's entire community or communities
- publish and distribute annual school profiles that include statements about school's values and priorities and statistical information about school and its communities

Supervisory Officers

- hold principals accountable for preparing and distributing school profiles and school report cards, and developing, implementing, monitoring and evaluating school improvement plans

Directors of Education

- be held accountable by board for preparing and distributing board report cards and developing, implementing, monitoring and evaluating board improvement plans

PUPILS

This section on pupils is included in a book on education governance, not because they are part of the governance structure (they are more the governed than governors), but because they are the ultimate intended beneficiaries of the system. They are at the same time the raison d'être of the whole exercise and the least powerful of its participants.[31]

Nowhere in the Constitution or in legislation will there be found reference to the rights of pupils, still less to a right to an education. Only two provinces have addressed this issue at all, and they only in the context of equal treatment.[32]

Many of the constitutions in American states, on the other hand, have provisions which have been interpreted as establishing a constitutional right to an education. The requirement of the State of Washington Constitution that the "legislature shall provide for a general and uniform system of public schools" and that the legislature has a "paramount duty" to "make ample provision for education of all children" has been held to confer on the children of Washington a constitutionally "guaranteed education" in which the first priority is to provide "fully sufficient funds". All children residing within Washington's borders "have a constitutionally paramount 'right' to be amply provided with an education", through a "general and uniform system of public schools".[33]

The argument for a constitutional right to an education has been made in Canada, asserting that, since the Charter expressly recognizes the right to denominational education (s. 29) and the right to minority language education (s. 23), it would seem strange to deny a more general right to education in the Charter. The courts in Ontario and Alberta have to date shown no disposition to accept these arguments.[34]

In Ontario, the emphasis remains on the obligations of pupils. They must:

(a) be diligent in attempting to master such studies as are part of the program in which they are enrolled;

(b) exercise self-discipline;

---

[31] The total extent of their participation in the power structure is their newly acquired right to representation on school boards. See Chapter 6 under heading "Pupil Representation on Boards".

[32] See *Saskatchewan Human Rights Code*, S.S. 1979, c. S.24.1 (as amended to 1993, c. 61), s. 13, and the Quebec *Charter of human rights and freedoms*, R.S.Q., c. C12, s. 40, which tamely provides that: "Every person has a right, to the extent and according to the standards provided for by law, to free public education."

[33] *Seattle School District No. 1 of King County v. State of Washington*, 90 Wash.2d 476, 585 P.2d 71 (1978). See, generally, Alexander, *American Public School Law*, 3rd ed. (St. Paul, Minn., West Publishing Co., 1992), Chapters 2 and 19.

[34] See W.A. MacKay, "The Elwood Case: Vindicating the Educational Rights of the Disabled", in (1987), 3 Can. J. Spec. Ed. 112.

    (c)   accept such discipline as would be exercised by a kind, firm, judicious parent;

    (d)   attend classes punctually and regularly;

    (e)   be courteous to fellow pupils, and obedient and courteous to teachers;

    (f)   be clean in person and habits;

    (g)   take tests and examinations as required or directed; and

    (h)   show respect for school property.[35]

Although the government's new funding system may be "student-focused", it is difficult to conclude that the governance structure is similarly focused.

---

[35] Reg. 298, s. 23.

9

Former Funding Model

BACKGROUND

A principal focus of education in the 19th century was local and (for Roman Catholics) denominational autonomy.[1] Denominational issues continued and still continue to play a prominent role in the politics of education and have more recently been joined by issues involving the language of education. However, one factor which has always been at the centre of discourse in the governance of all aspects of education is money. In the 20th century, the raising and distribution of revenue has been a central concern of education fiscal policy.

Until Bill 160, the funding of education in the province was a shared local and provincial responsibility. Revenue came from two main sources: local property taxes set by local school boards; and grants to school boards by the province.

In the 19th century, school boards had been financed primarily from local resources and they received grants from the province based on the number of pupils. In the 20th century, the province came to play a continually expanding role in education finance.

School boards continued to have significant autonomy in the establishment of their own policies, priorities and expenditure, and the raising of money for those purposes. Grants were made to local school boards by the province related to that expenditure to ensure the maintenance of adequate standards of education throughout the province.

Autonomy and equality are, in practice, inconsistent values. Autonomy, self-government, necessarily includes the power to make decisions independently of the decisions of others. The power to make decisions is determined by the ability to implement them. The power to make decisions on the spending of money is limited or enhanced by the resources available to carry them out. The

---

[1] See F.A. Walker, *Catholic Education and Politics in Ontario*, vol. I (Toronto, Federation of Catholic Education Associations of Ontario, 1976).

results will be unequal. This is as true of school boards as it is for nation states and the political subdivisions thereof.

Until recently, provincial policy has been marked by continuing and varied attempts to reconcile local autonomy with equity to ensure that pupils throughout the province have equal opportunity while at the same time enabling communities to take their own varying needs and resources into account in their decisions on education. As long as the power to raise money locally remains, the variations in local wealth will produce unequal results.

VARIATIONS IN ASSESSMENT WEALTH

The inequities resulting from unequal assessment wealth was one of the main criticisms of a funding model based on local control. School boards with a rich assessment base were able to spend considerably more money per pupil than assessment-poor school boards, with a similar or lower tax effort. The ability to raise revenue did not necessarily coincide with the educational needs.

The uneven distribution of the tax base across the province and its results were described in the Ontario Fair Tax Commission report:

> School boards that operate in jurisdictions with access to large tax bases relative to the size of the student population they serve are able to raise revenue more easily than boards that operate in jurisdictions without access to large tax bases. Why should some students be deprived of services because they happen to live in an assessment-poor school district?
>
> There are enormous disparities in equalized assessment per pupil among the 114 school boards that operate both elementary and secondary schools on a permanent basis.
>
> The numbers indicate clearly that there are wide disparities in residential and commercial and industrial assessment bases both between the public and separate systems and within each system.
>
> There are also wide variations in equalized assessment per pupil between public and separate boards that serve the same community . . . The provincial grants system is supposed to compensate for differences in per pupil assessment base, but it is only partly effective.[2]

The first attempts to take into account variations in the local ability to raise taxes was in relation to rural boards in 1910 and extended to urban boards in 1924. By 1930, all legislative grants were apportioned to boards on the basis of local property assessment and actual expenditures by boards. In 1936, secondary schools received grants based on teachers' salaries, attendance and assessment.

After the Second World War, the amount of the grants increased and the concept was introduced of "approved costs", that is, the part of the amounts

---

[2] *Report of the Ontario Fair Tax Commission* (1993), p. 602.

spent by boards which the province would pay for. The next step in 1958 was to establish equalized taxable assessment to mitigate the effect of local variations in assessment practice.

The "Foundation Plan" of 1963 introduced equalization grants to ensure that every board received sufficient revenue for its educational program while maintaining its fiscal responsibility. For a short time in the 1970s, the government imposed "expenditure ceilings" to limit the amounts which boards could raise locally without losing an equivalent amount of grant. These ceilings were abolished in 1976 and thereafter most boards spent above the provincially approved levels by resorting to local assessment. One could conclude from this phenomenon that the provincial grants had too low a ceiling. Disparities in local assessment continued to be a problem.

In its report, the Macdonald Commission in 1985 concluded that because above-ceiling expenditures were paid for from local assessment:

> Less affluent boards are frustrated in trying to match the level of programs and services, including contractual agreements, set by the assessment-rich boards. Yet because of the initiatives taken by a few assessment-rich boards, there are higher expectations across the Province.[3]

The commission's proposed remedy, that expenditures above grant levels be refinanced solely from residential and farm assessment, was not pursued. However, the commission's recommendations on a more equitable distribution of the assessment of the property of corporations were implemented in 1989.[4]

One remedy that gained support was based on the sharing or "pooling" of local tax revenues, either among coterminous boards or province-wide. In 1992, the report of the Property Tax Working Group of the Fair Tax Commission, however, rejected any provincial pooling of local assessment as a solution. Its view was that such an approach would breach school board accountability to its local taxpayers and involve revenue raised in one local jurisdiction being spent in other jurisdictions. The report's solution was to reduce dependence on property tax as a source of revenue for education and increase provincial transfers and equalization payments to offset inequities.

The Report of the Fair Tax Commission itself went further. Its report recommended that local commercial and industrial property tax for education be replaced with a provincial commercial and industrial property tax levied at a uniform rate and that education residential property taxes be replaced with funding from provincial general revenues, primarily personal income tax.

No one solution received widespread approval. No remedy could please both the haves and the have-nots. It is significant that the last report before the

---

[3] *Report of the Commission on Financing of Elementary and Secondary Education in Ontario* (1985), at p. 59.

[4] See amendments made to ss. 112 and 113 of the *Education Act* by S.O. 1992, c. 17 (since repealed by S.O. 1997, c. 31).

reforms of Bill 104 and Bill 160, that of the Education Finance Reform Working Group established by the Minister, was unable to reach a consensus.

On the one hand, public school interests maintained that school boards should have access to their local property tax base in order to meet local needs and be accountable to their taxpayers, and that money raised locally should not be spent in other jurisdictions. There was also an underlying current of feeling in many quarters that the public system, because of its universal accessibility and its vital role in ensuring an education to every person in the province, need feel no guilt because of its position of primacy. This view was perceived by others as inconsistent with the values of equality and minority rights now constitutionally entrenched in the *Canadian Charter of Rights and Freedoms*. Separate school interests and French-language associations, feeling particularly disadvantaged under the existing regime, supported provincial pooling of commercial and industrial assessment, access of local school boards to residential assessment and requiring all taxpayers to designate residential school support with undesignated residential assessment to be pooled according to pupil attendance.

Despite the reforms which had been made piecemeal since the beginning of the century, there is no doubt that there was a compelling need for action on the problems with the existing funding model which remained. The main issues were the continued reliance on local assessment with its variations from board to board and the consequent disparities in board spending, the competition between public and separate boards for assessment revenues and the failure so far of provincial plans to remedy these problems to everyone's satisfaction.

VARIATIONS IN SPENDING

Even after the application of the provincial equalization factors, the total assessment per pupil in 1996 (residential and commercial and industrial combined) varied from a high of $495,398 for the richest board (Metropolitan Toronto School Board) to $100,091 for the poorest board (Kirkland Lake-Timiskaming Roman Catholic Separate School Board) — a ratio of about 5 to 1. This meant that the richest board was able to make over-ceiling expenditures five times greater than the poorest board with the same mill rate.

There was a strong relationship between assessment wealth per student and actual spending per student above the ceiling. However, school boards made their own decisions on the extent to which they taxed their assessment base to raise above-ceiling revenues. Obviously, it was easier for an assessment-rich board to spend significantly over ceiling than it was for an assessment-poor board. As a result, there were considerable variations in above-ceiling expenditures. Although the legal rights of taxation and provincial support were uniform throughout the province, political and economic factors influenced their exercise to produce results far from uniform.

COMPETITION FOR LOCAL TAX REVENUES

Because of the crucial part of local tax revenue in the overall scheme to enable boards to meet educational needs as they perceived them and the limits placed on that revenue by finite resources and local politics, coterminous boards had to compete for that revenue.

The issue of competition among boards for property tax revenues was noted by the Ontario Fair Tax Commission:

> One manifestation of this pressure (matching tax rates between coterminous boards) has been intense competition among neighbouring boards for school support and therefore assessment. A growing class of local officials devoted entirely to "assessment wars" with other boards has been created in public, separate, English and French boards across Ontario. This effort serves no purpose other than to shift resources from board to board, to the benefit of some students and the detriment of others. We consider this activity to be wasteful and destructive to the local cooperation that is essential to make the system perform better and deliver its services more efficiently.[5]

The competition arose from two factors:

(i) the existence in each jurisdiction of at least two boards, public and Roman Catholic; and

(ii) the constitutional right of Roman Catholics to choose between two boards, to designate their taxes to the separate school board or allow them to go to the public board.

Although there were no limits imposed by law on the level of tax rates imposed or amount of revenue raised, there were practical limits which had a significant impact on the tax rates actually set by school boards in the province. In order to retain the tax support of Roman Catholics, separate school boards had to set their tax rates to match public school board tax rates in virtually all areas of the province. In most cases, the rates were set slightly below public school board rates. To achieve this objective, separate school boards had to maximize their tax base: the greater the source of revenue, the lower the rate which would have to be imposed on it. If separate school board rates were set higher than those of the public board, there was an economic incentive for taxpayers to switch their designation to the public system. The direct effect of this was to reduce the assessment base available to a separate board. Setting a significantly higher tax rate than the public board could result in a decline in the total revenue of a separate board if a large number of Roman Catholics changed their designation in order to pay less.

---

[5] *Supra*, footnote 2, at pp. 684-5.

The financial incentive to change designation from the separate board to the public board was particularly influential on Roman Catholics who did not have school-aged children attending separate school. Taxpayers with children at school might be less influenced by their tax bill. It could be outweighed by their commitment to a Roman Catholic education and the right to vote for separate trustees.

The pressure on separate school boards to match the mill rates of public school boards and the relatively poorer assessment bases of separate school boards resulted in significant differences in above-ceiling expenditure by separate boards. Public boards had a higher above-ceiling ordinary expenditure per pupil than the coterminous separate board.

The problems of the York Region Roman Catholic Separate School Board in the early 1990s illustrate this problem. This board experienced financial difficulties in the late 1980s which resulted in an accumulated deficit in 1993-94. To return to financial stability, the board was required by the Ministry to levy successively higher tax rates each year over a five-year period. As separate school board tax rates exceeded public school board tax rates, the pupil residential assessment base of the separate board declined.

This experience confirmed the view of the Fair Tax Commission that "where public and separate boards in the same jurisdiction have very different fiscal capacities . . . [t]he pressure to [harmonize] residential tax rates will result in less being spent on the education of students in a poorer board than on students in a wealthier board serving the same geographical area".[6]

ROLE OF PROVINCIAL GRANTS

As the capacity to levy taxes varied widely among school board jurisdictions, one of the principal purposes of provincial grants was to equalize the burden of the costs of education across the province. The purpose of the grants was to ensure that all pupils, wherever they lived, should have equal access to an acceptable level of education.

The grant rates were set to mitigate the consequences of the variations in resources. Consequently, the less money a board could raise through local assessment, the higher the grant from the province and *vice versa*.

The provincial grants were governed by the Provincial Equalization Grant Plan, first introduced in 1969. The province established a per pupil expenditure ceiling, or "recognized expenditure", which was the cost to provide education at a base level in each local board area.

The first step under the grant plan was to "equalize" school board revenues throughout the province to a prescribed limit known as "recognized ordinary

---

[6] *Ibid.*, at p. 684.

expenditures". A board's "recognized ordinary expenditure" for the "basic per pupil grant" (Category 1 under the grant regulations),[7] was the grant ceiling times the number of pupils. The province in effect guaranteed that every school board would have sufficient per pupil revenues to meet the provincially recognized ordinary expenditures and thus be able to provide an acceptable level of education. In 1996, the province set recognized ordinary expenditures at $4,028 for each elementary student and $4,920 for each secondary student.

The amount of the provincial equalizing grant was the difference between the amount of recognized ordinary expenditures and the amount which the board could raise from local taxes by applying a provincially uniform mill rate (the "standard mill rate") to the assessment of property taxable for the purposes of the school board. The assessment base was adjusted to equalize variations in methods of assessment around the province ("equalized assessment base"). Put another way, a board's provincial grant for recognized expenditure (the basic per pupil grant), was the board's total recognized expenditure (the grant ceiling times the number of pupils), minus the amount resulting from the application of the provincial equalized mill rate to the board's equalized assessment base.

The equalized assessment base was determined by the application of an assessment equalization factor. This was arrived at by comparing sales prices of property within each local jurisdiction over the preceding year with the local assessed value for each of nine identified classes of property. An equalization factor was then determined for each municipality to adjust its assessment base to an "equalized" assessment value. The application of the standard mill rate to the equalized assessment base was intended to ensure that taxpayers would make the same proportionate contribution or "tax effort" towards the provision of the basic level of education.

In addition to the grants provided for the base level of expenditure (recognized ordinary expenditure), boards received a number of special purpose grants to recognize the higher costs associated with particular geographic, demographic and socio-economic conditions of a board as well as specific programs and services. The special purpose grants under the annual general legislative grants were:

Category 2: board specific grants (to offset geographic, demographic or socio-economic differences in the cost of providing the base level of education with specific grants for goods and services, small schools, small boards, small sections, French-as-a-first language, compensatory education and declining enrolment)

---

[7] See, *e.g.*, *General Legislative Grants, 1996*, O. Reg. 116/96 (as amended to O. Reg. 162/96).

Category 3: program specific grants (for mandated programs or to assist with the adoption of new provincial initiatives such as class size reductions in Grades 1 and 2 and to implement other programs to respond to local needs)

Category 4: capital projects grants (for projects such as building new schools and additions, purchasing sites and replacing or renovating existing schools)

Category 5: additional provincial support

SPENDING ABOVE GRANT CEILINGS

Because of equalizing grants, assessment wealth was irrelevant to board revenues up to the level of recognized expenditures. However, boards were free to provide services above this base level, funded exclusively from the local property tax base, and most boards in the province did spent above the provincially established grant ceilings. Assessment wealth was the main factor in spending above the grant ceilings.

The equalizing grant provided sufficient revenue to meet the standard of recognized ordinary expenditures. If a board's actual mill rate exceeded the standard mill rate, the actual revenues would exceed the level required for recognized ordinary expenditures. As a result, boards were able to make expenditures above recognized ordinary expenditures. These additional expenditures were known as "over-ceiling expenditures". The ability to raise funds for over-ceiling expenditures varied widely from board to board depending on the assessment wealth of the board. Equalization grants played no role in the amount of this spending.

NEGATIVE GRANTS ISSUE

Two school boards in the former board structure and under the old funding model were characterized as "negative grant boards". They were the public boards in Metropolitan Toronto and Ottawa. Both cities had high concentrations of assessment wealth.

Within Metropolitan Toronto and Ottawa, the provincial standard mill rate applied to the public school per pupil equalized assessment produced an amount greater than the province's per pupil recognized expenditure (the grant ceiling). The difference between these amounts, or the excess in equalized local per pupil tax revenue over the grant ceiling, was what was referred to by the province as the negative grant.

The Metropolitan Toronto public boards and the Ottawa Board of Education, having the wealthiest equalized assessment bases in the province, were able to raise with the same tax effort greater over-ceiling revenue than other boards. This resulted in problems for coterminous boards. The Metropolitan Separate School Board operated schools in the same jurisdiction as the metropolitan public boards and the Ottawa Roman Catholic Separate School Board and the Ottawa-Carleton French-language boards operated schools in the same jurisdiction as the Ottawa Board of Education (English public). These coterminous boards had to compete with the public boards in the delivery of programs and services for their pupils. It was difficult for the separate boards which did not have the same assessment wealth to retain students when the assessment-rich board could offer better facilities and programs.

Three other boards, the Muskoka Board of Education, the Haliburton Board of Education and the West Parry Sound Board of Education (all public English) were also approaching negative grant status.

The public boards in Metropolitan Toronto did not actually "collect" the amount of the negative grant. It was an "artificial" calculation flowing from the formulae contained in the province's equalization model. The school board raised property taxes in excess of its imputed grant position with reference solely to the level of educational services actually provided. It did not actually have cash in hand at the end of the year equal to the provincially calculated negative grant. Payment of the negative grant amount to the province would have required the school board either to raise additional revenues by increasing the mill rate or to reduce services.

The province's position was that, because of Metropolitan Toronto's public boards relatively strong property tax base, as reflected in its negative grant position, the taxpayers had less of a burden than taxpayers in other jurisdictions in raising revenues for the basic per pupil expenditure (grant) ceiling. The province asserted that, if the amount of the negative grant was paid to the province, the taxpayers would then be paying an equitable share of the basic education cost for the whole province, through distribution of the money to other boards in the province.

In view of the hostile reaction of Metropolitan Toronto trustees and taxpayers to the idea of raising taxes in Toronto to fund education in, say, Timiskaming, and their refusal to "write a cheque to the province", the province was reluctant to try to compel payment. There were also rumblings that such a payment would be an "indirect tax" on taxpayers in Metropolitan Toronto and therefore beyond provincial constitutional authority.

Instead, the province amended the Act[8] to enable a board to enter into an agreement with the Minister to make an "equalization contribution" to the province up to the amount of the negative grant. However, no such agreement was ever entered into and no cheques were written to the province. The issue remained unresolved.

---

[8] S.O. 1996, c. 13, s. 9.

POOLING

One reform of the former funding model which was implemented provided for the phasing in, between 1989 and 1995, of "pooling" among coterminous boards of the commercial and industrial assessment wealth of "designated ratepayers". These were defined as publicly traded corporations and Crown corporations, among other types of commercial and industrial taxpayers. Initially, the pooled commercial and industrial assessment was shared between public and separate boards on the basis of each board's share of residential and farm assessment. This was later extended, from 1996 to 1998, and shared on the basis of enrolment. This reform was not fully implemented as it was pre-empted by Bill 160.

PROVINCIAL INTERVENTION

The Macdonald Commission report concluded that the mill rate equalization plan introduced in 1978 had been successful in equalizing the incidence of local burden up to the ceiling or "approved" levels of expenditure but stated:

> However, for school boards that incur expenditures beyond those levels [of the recognized ordinary expenditure] the financing of such expenditures becomes the responsibility of the local school boards. It is at this level that the concept of equalization fails because the local wealth of school boards, measured by their equalized assessment per pupil, varies widely. The levying of one equalized mill by an assessment-rich board generates a level of tax revenues per pupil several times greater than that generated by an assessment-poor board levying the same equalized mill.[9]

The commission's solution was total funding by the province. It felt that total funding would present the greatest scope for equalizing educational opportunities and would lend itself to a program-funding approach. It noted that various forms of provincialization are in effect in other provinces. However given the administrative and political realities of Ontario, the commission did not see full provincial funding as a viable option for the immediate future.

Ten years later, however, the Ontario Fair Tax Commission based its report on the principles that:

- Since all Ontarians are equally entitled to education experiences that support lifelong learning, the ability of education systems to provide those experiences should not vary according to the amount of money that can be raised locally.

---

[9] *Supra*, footnote 3, at p. 55.

- The distribution of centrally allocated funds for publicly supported education should vary only according to geographical or demographic variations in the costs of meeting needs fairly and equitably.[10]

Accordingly, the majority report recommended that:

> The Provincial government should assume responsibility for the funding of education to a Provincial standard, allocating funds to school boards based on per student cost, student needs, and community characteristics which affect education costs, such as poverty and language.[11]

The key words in this recommendation are "community characteristics". The issue is not what are community characteristics, but who is given the power to determine what they are. One solution which was canvassed was to move funding to the province but to retain some form of limited autonomy. The majority report of the Fair Tax Commission sought to achieve this with a recommendation that school boards should be permitted to raise additional funds for "discretionary spending" through a local levy on the residential property tax base. This local levy would be restricted to a fixed percentage of 10% or less of the total amount of provincial funding provided to the board.

The 1994 report of the Royal Commission on Learning made the same recommendations (equal per pupil funding determined at the provincial level plus board discretion to spend up to 10% above that amount, to be raised from residential assessment only).

Similarly, the government's advisory panel recommended in 1996 that education's reliance on the residential property tax be reduced but not eliminated:

> The residential property tax support for education should be continued, but it should be raised according to a Provincially set uniform tax rate. This tax should be collected by municipalities and forwarded to the school boards.
>
> School boards should be able to access the residential tax base further in order to raise additional revenues of up to 5 per cent of their approved budgets.[12]

In a spirited dissenting report, Professor Neil Brooks of the Osgoode Hall Law School disagreed with the recommendation that school boards should be permitted to raise up to 10% additional funds from the local tax base. He stated:

> The present Ontario system of school finance is inequitable, irrational, a blatant denial of equal educational opportunity, and an egregious anomaly in a province committed to liberal ideals. Students living in the wealthiest and most advantaged communities have much greater educational resources than students living in the

---

[10] *Supra*, footnote 2, at p. 674.

[11] *Ibid.*, at p. 677.

[12] Letter from the Who Does What Advisory Panel (appointed by the province and chaired by D. Crombie), to the Minister of Municipal Affairs and Housing and the Minister of Education and Training (December 23, 1996).

poorest communities. In an economy that is indisputably Provincial in character, we continue to treat educational funding as a predominantly local function. In a culture in which we devote more money to schooling than almost any other government function, hardly anyone outside a small band of initiates understands how schools are financed.

In short, there is no case for allowing educational funding to vary at all between schools based upon the capacity or effort of local taxpayers.[13]

This approach won the day. The funding model introduced by the government under Bill 160 made no provision for local levies by school boards.

PROVINCE'S DECISION

A number of factors went into the government's solution:

- a stated belief that spending by school boards was excessive
- a perception that too much was being spent on administration and other out-of-classroom activities
- reports of inadequate education achievement
- a general desire to reduce costs and taxes
- a policy of realignment of the services provided for by various levels of government
- a conviction that greater control at the centre was necessary to achieve these objectives

Accordingly, the stated aims of the government's reform package included:

- a shift of resources to increase "classroom spending"
- "student-focused" funding
- education funding placed under provincial control
- provincial control over spending
- increased accountability to taxpayers, parents and the government
- provision of funds for school construction only where a provincially determined need was established

On March 25, 1998, the Minister of Education and Training announced the new "student-focused" funding formula:

In addition to defining and protecting classroom spending for the first time, this new fair approach to funding will ensure that each and every student will have the same opportunity to acquire the skills and expertise they need . . .

This has not always been the case. Under previous governments, per pupil spending varied dramatically from board to board. Some students have been denied an equal opportunity to learn, simply because their boards lacked access to a larger assessment base.

---

[13] *Minority Report* (Ontario Fair Tax Commission, 1993), pp. 1017-18.

Each and every student in Ontario deserves the best education our province can give him or her — this idea provides the spirit and the basis of today's announcement of Ontario's new, student-focused approach to funding.[14]

The new funding approach was put into place for the 1998-99 fiscal year.

---

[14] *Student-Focused Funding for Ontario: A Guide Book* (Toronto, Ministry of Education and Training, March, 1998).

10

New Funding Model: Tax Revenue

PART IX OF EDUCATION ACT

The new funding model is implemented partly through a new part of the Act[1] and partly by executive action through the annual legislative grants regulation and the setting of tax rates by the Minister of Finance. The Act contains the new method of raising revenue; regulations will prescribe the amount of and how the boards may spend the revenue.

The former Part IX of the Act, which was repealed and replaced by Bill 160, consisted of 29 sections. It had no subdivisions. It dealt with board auditors, debentures, board estimates, regulations for apportionment of grants, determination, assessment and collection of rates by boards, borrowing and the taxation of trailers.

The new Part IX contains 133 sections, separated into Divisions A to F. Division A, "General", deals with estimates, board support, school rates in certain circumstances, borrowing and investment by boards, financial administration of boards and some miscellaneous matters.

Division B, "Education Taxes", contains the system presently in operation for the levying and collection of the taxes which are to be determined by regulations made by the Minister of Finance.

Division C, "Taxes Set by Boards", confers powers on boards to determine and collect rates on rateable property. Division C is "inoperative".

Division D, "Supervision of Boards' Financial Affairs", provides for the investigation and supervision of a board's financial affairs when a board is in financial difficulty.

Division E, "Education Development Charges", contains new provisions for education development charges (often called "lot levies"), which enable boards to recover education land costs from developments which increase the demand for pupil accommodation.

---

[1] See Part IX, "Finance".

117

Division F, "Review of Education Funding", makes Division C "inoperative" and provides for a future review of education funding.

SOURCES OF REVENUE

Under the new funding model, there are five sources from which district school boards can derive revenue:

    (i)   residential property tax revenue from their own school supporters;

   (ii)   business property tax revenue shared between coterminous boards on the basis of student enrolment;

 (iii)   provincial grants, which equalize board disparities in revenues;

 (iv)   education development charges; and

  (v)   other sources, such as tuition fees from non-residents and the rental, lease or sale of surplus properties.

NEW STRUCTURE FOR PROPERTY TAX REVENUE

For the purposes of revenue from property taxes, property is divided into two categories: residential property; and business property. In each case, the tax rates imposed on the properties are now fixed by the Minister of Finance but there are different rules for setting the tax rates applicable to each category of property.

As taxes on residential property are the only taxes distributed to boards according to ratepayer designation, the rules for designation by partnerships and corporations, public and private, are applicable only to residential property. The elements of the new system are accordingly:

    (i)   the category of property subject to taxation;

   (ii)   designation of board support for residential property taxes;

 (iii)   the setting of the tax rates for each category of property; and

 (iv)   the method of distribution among boards of the taxes raised on each category of property.

PROPERTY SUBJECT TO TAXATION

The basic principle is that all real property which is liable to assessment and taxation under the *Assessment Act*[2] is taxable for school purposes unless spe-

---

[2] R.S.O. 1990, c. A.31 (as amended to 1998, c. 33).

cifically exempted by legislation. Property is divided into two categories, residential and business, and each category is treated differently.

"Residential property" is property in the residential/farm property class, the farmlands property class, the managed forests property class or the multiresidential property class, all as prescribed under the *Assessment Act*. In addition, other classes of real property not listed in s. 7(2) of the *Assessment Act* may be prescribed as "residential property" by the Minister of Finance.[3]

The new multi-residential property class prescribed under the *Assessment Act* is the only class of property which is prescribed for this purpose.[4] However, in making regulations prescribing classes of property as "residential property", the Minister of Finance is not limited in the exercise of his or her discretion by the use of "residential" in the statutory definition.[5] "Business property" is defined in the Act[6] as property in the commercial property class, the industrial property class or the pipeline property class, all as prescribed under the *Assessment Act*. Also included as "business property" are specified types of property which are taxed under the *Municipal Act*: the roadway and rights of way of a railway company; and land owned and used as a transmission or distribution corridor by power utilities prescribed by the Minister of Finance.[7] In addition, the Minister of Finance may by regulation prescribe as "business property" classes of property other than those listed in s. 7(2) of the *Assessment Act*. The following classes of property have been prescribed:

   (i)   the office building property class;
  (ii)   the shopping centre property class;
 (iii)   the parking lots and vacant land property class; and
 (iv)   the large industrial property class.[8]

---

[3] *Education Act*, ss. 257.5, 257.12(1)(a). Section 7(2) of the *Assessment Act* provides:
    7(2) The classes prescribed by the Minister shall include, but are not restricted to, the following:
    1. The residential/farm property class.
    2. The multi-residential property class.
    3. The commercial property class.
    4. The industrial property class.
    5. The pipe line property class.
    6. The farmlands property class.
    7. The managed forests property class.
    Note, however, that s. 7(3) provides: "Nothing in subsection (2) restricts the discretion of the Minister to define which is included in a class."
[4] See *Tax Matters — Definition of Business Property and Residential Property*, O. Reg. 394/98, s. 2.
[5] *Education Act*, s. 257.12(2).
[6] Section 257.5.
[7] *Municipal Act*, R.S.O. 1990, c. M.45 (as amended to 1998, c. 33), s. 368.3.
[8] See footnote 3, *supra*.

However, in making regulations prescribing classes of property as "business property", the Minister of Finance is not limited in the exercise of his or her discretion by the use of "business" in the statutory definition. The only express limitation on this power is that the Minister cannot use the school support of persons assessed to define a class of real property.[9]

If a particular property consists of different classes of property, the assessment commissioner determines the share of the value attributable to each class and assesses the property according to the proportion each share constitutes of the total value and includes each proportion on the assessment roll.[10]

DESIGNATION OF BOARD SUPPORT FOR RESIDENTIAL TAX PURPOSES[11]

An individual who is an owner or tenant of residential property in the area of jurisdiction of a board (or in the case of an English-language public board, outside the area of jurisdiction of all boards but within a municipality), is entitled on application under the *Assessment Act* to the assessment commissioner[12] for the area in which the property is located to have his or her name included or altered in the assessment roll as a supporter of the board in accordance with the following rules:

English-language public board: any individual
English-language Roman Catholic board: an individual who is a Roman Catholic
French-language public board: an individual who is a French-language rights holder
French-language separate board: an individual who is a Roman Catholic and a French-language rights holder
Protestant separate school board: an individual who is Protestant in a municipality in which there is a Protestant separate school board

If no application for school support is received and approved by the assessment commissioner to the contrary, the assessment commissioner must indicate on the assessment roll that a person is an English-language public board supporter if that person is entitled to be such a supporter under the *Education Act*.

---

[9] *Education Act*, s. 257.12(9).
[10] *Assessment Act*, s. 14(5), added by S.O. 1997, c. 5, s. 9(3).
[11] *Education Act*, ss. 236-239.
[12] In the *Assessment Act*, "assessment commissioner" has been replaced by "assessment corporation" (S.O. 1997, c. 43, Sch. G, s. 18), but "assessment commissioner" remains in the *Education Act*.

Designations of board support for residential property may also be made by partnerships and private corporations. A partnership or a private corporation may require that the whole or any part of residential property which it owns be assessed for the purposes of Roman Catholic boards (English or French) or French-language public boards. Any part of the assessment not so designated is assessed for English-language public board purposes.

In the case of a corporation, the part of the assessment specifically designated cannot exceed the percentage of all the shares of the corporation held by supporters of the board designated other than the English-language public board; in the case of a partnership, the percentage interest in the partnership held by supporters of the board designated other than the English-language public board. Thus, for example, in the case of a private corporation, the portions of an assessment of a corporation that are assessed for English-language Roman Catholic board purposes cannot bear a greater proportion to the whole assessment of the corporation than the number of shares held in the corporation by supporters of an English-language Roman Catholic board bears to the total number of shares of the corporation issued and outstanding.

No designations of board support are made by "designated ratepayers".[13]

ASSESSMENT ROLLS

It is the responsibility of the assessment commissioner [corporation] to prepare an assessment roll for each municipality, which contains details of every property including with respect to taxation for education purposes:

(i)   the name of every tenant who is a supporter of a school board;
(ii) the classification of the property;
(iii) if a person is a French-language rights holder;
(iv) religion if Roman Catholic;
(v)   type of school board the person supports under the *Education Act*; and
(vi) whether a corporation is a "designated ratepayer" under the *Education Act*.

In the preparation of the assessment roll, the assessment commissioner, in determining the names and school support of persons, is guided by the applications received and approved by the assessment commissioner and by the notices of designation of school support. The assessment commissioner each year prepares a list showing the name of every person who is entitled to support a school board and the type of school board he or she supports for each munici-

---

[13] Defined in s. 238(1). A more appropriate term would have been "non-designating ratepayers".

pality or locality in the commissioner's assessment region, and delivers the list to the secretary of each school board in the municipality or locality on or before September 30.

RESIDENTIAL PROPERTY TAXES

Instead of tax mill rates set by local boards, the Minister of Finance now has sole power to set the tax rate to be applied to the residential assessment base of each municipality for the purpose of raising revenue.[14] With two specific exceptions, the regulations must prescribe a single tax rate for the residential/farm property class and the multi-residential property class.

The first exception is contained in amendments to the *Municipal Act* made in 1997 which enable the Minister of Finance by regulation to reduce the tax rates otherwise payable by prescribed percentages on certain subclasses of property, including farm land awaiting development for residential/farm and multi-residential purposes.[15] The second exception is that the tax rate for the farmlands property class and the managed forests property class is 25% of the tax rate prescribed for the residential/farm property class.[16]

The residential rate is applied to the assessment of residential property in a municipality and the amounts levied are collected by the municipality on behalf of the board. The levied amount is forwarded to the school board designated by the occupant of the residential property. Thus, taxes from residential property collected from self-designated English-language separate school supporters are forwarded only to the English-language district separate school board serving that municipality. The same principle applies with respect to taxes from English-language public school supporters, French-language separate school supporters and French-language public school supporters.[17]

Amounts levied on property of a partnership or a private corporation that is taxable for the purposes of one or more boards is distributed in accordance with the proportions of its assessment that result from the application of the rules applicable to partnerships and private corporations. As residential property tax revenue is distributed to school boards on the basis of taxpayer designation, the per pupil revenues from this source will vary among the school boards serving the same municipality. These variations will be due to variations in the number of supporters and the assessment base associated with those supporters, and to variations in the ratio of student population to supporters. These variations in per pupil funding are not equalized in this part of the model.

---

14 Section 257.12(1), (6).
15 *Municipal Act*, s. 368.1(1), (2).
16 *Education Act*, s. 257.12(5).
17 Section 257.9.

Adjustments to equalize per pupil revenue are provided for under the grant part of the model.

Where a district school board serves more than one municipality, all municipalities served must levy, collect and pay the appropriate share of taxes from residential property to the appropriate school board. The rules relating to the designation of board support and distribution of taxes based on those designations do not apply to "designated ratepayers".[18] The taxes levied on residential property of a designated ratepayer are distributed in the same manner as is provided for rates levied on business property of the designated ratepayer.

"DESIGNATED RATEPAYERS"

A "designated ratepayer" is defined in s. 238(1) to include:

(a) the Crown in right of Canada or a province,

(b) a corporation without share capital or corporation sole[19] that is an agency, board or commission of the Crown in right of Canada or a province,

(c) a municipal corporation,

(d) a corporation without share capital that is a local board as defined in the *Municipal Affairs Act*,

(e) a conservation authority established by or under the *Conservation Authorities Act* or a predecessor of that Act, or

(f) a public corporation.

A "public corporation" is defined in s. 238(1) to include:

(a) a body corporate that is, by reason of its shares, a reporting issuer within the meaning of the *Securities Act* or that has, by reason of its shares, a status comparable to a reporting issuer under the law of any other jurisdiction,

(b) a body corporate that issues shares that are traded on any market if the prices at which they are traded on that market are regularly published in a newspaper or business or financial publication of general and regular paid circulation, or

(c) a body corporate that is, within the meaning of [provisions] of the *Securities Act*, controlled by or is a subsidiary of a public corporation . . .

---

[18] *Supra*, footnote 13.

[19] Corporations sole were originally mainly ecclesiastical. An archbishop, bishop, dean, parson and vicar are all corporations sole. The Sovereign is also a corporation sole at common law and in England some Ministers of the Crown have been made corporations sole by statute. The consequence of being a corporation sole is that official property passes on the holder's death to the successor in office as if the corporation sole and the successor were the same person.

Designated ratepayers do not make designations of tax support for boards. Taxes payable by designated taxpayers on both residential property and business property are distributed in accordance with pupil enrolment.

BUSINESS PROPERTY TAXES

Bill 160 enabled the Minister of Finance by regulation to set the tax rates on business property.[20] This power was subsequently extended to include the prescribing of rates for the purpose of calculating payments in lieu of taxes under s. 361.1 of the *Municipal Act* for property exempt from taxation for school purposes.

Business property taxes differ from taxes on residential property taxes in three respects:

1. There is no designation of board support.
2. The taxes are distributed in accordance with pupil enrolment.
3. Unlike the tax rate on residential property, there may be variations in the tax rate on business property.

The Minister may prescribe different tax rates for:

    (a) different municipalities;
    (b) different parts of a municipality, as specified in an Act, regulation or order implementing municipal restructuring;[21]
    (c) different parts of territory without municipal organization[22] including those deemed to be attached to a municipality for purposes related to taxation or deemed by statute to be a locality;

---

[20] Section 257.12(1), as extended by the *Fairness for Property Taxpayers Act, 1998*, S.O. 1998, c. 33, s. 42(1). For an alternative method of raising revenue on business property, which enables the Minister of Finance to requisition the amounts to be raised by taxation by municipalities, see discussion later in this section.

[21] "Restructuring" is defined in s. 25.2(1) of the *Municipal Act* as:
    (a) annexing part of a municipality to another municipality,
    (b) annexing a locality that does not form part of a municipality to a municipality,
    (c) amalgamating a municipality with another municipality,
    (d) separating a local municipality from a county for municipal purposes,
    (e) joining a local municipality to a county for municipal purposes,
    (f) dissolving all or part of a municipality, and
    (g) incorporating the inhabitants of a locality as a municipality.

[22] *I.e.*, territory without municipal organization and deemed by virtue of regulation made by Cabinet under s. 56 or s. 58.1(2) of the Act to be within the area of jurisdiction of a school authority. See *Territory Without Municipal Organization Attached to a District Municipality*, R.R.O. 1990, Reg. 311.

(d) different classes of property prescribed by the regulations under the Act or the *Assessment Act*;

(e) different subclasses of real property prescribed by the regulations made under the *Assessment Act*;

(f) real property on any basis on which a municipality or Ontario is permitted to set different tax rates for real property for municipal purposes;

(g) different portions of a property's assessment;

(h) different geographic areas established for certain purposes;[23] and

(i) different parts of a municipality based on whether or not the parts are in the area of jurisdiction of an English-language public board.[24]

As a result of amendments made to the Act by the *Fairness for Property Taxpayers Act, 1998*,[25] the authority of the Minister of Finance to prescribe tax rates on business property and to requisition amounts of business taxes from municipalities has to be exercised in compliance with specified rules related to the "weighted average tax rate" for school purposes for commercial classes and industrial classes of business property. The rules set out the method for determining the weighted average tax rate,[26] and provide that the rate for the year 2005 and later years must not exceed 3.3%.[27]

The rules also provide for the consequences of weighted average tax rates being more or less than 3.3% in any of the years 1998 to 2004, inclusive. If the rate in the year previous to any of those years was 3.3% or less, the rate for the current year cannot exceed 3.3%.[28] If the rate in the year previous to any year was more than 3.3%, the rate for the current year cannot exceed a prescribed maximum, calculated as: the rate for the previous year minus the excess of the rate over 3.3%, divided by the number of years from the current year to 2005.[29] For example, if the rate in the year 2000 was 4.1%, the rate for the year 2001 would be 4.1% minus 0.8% divided by 4 years (0.2%), that is, 3.9%. The same calculation would be made for the following years, so that by the year 2004, the rate has been reduced to 3.3%.

Amendments to the Act made by the *Small Business and Charities Protection Act*[30] provide for a different method of raising and levying taxes on business property. Under those amendments, the Minister of Finance may requisition amounts for a year from an upper-tier municipality or a single-tier

---

[23] *I.e.*, for the purposes of s. 368.3(1), paras. 1 and 2 of the *Municipal Act*.

[24] *Education Act*, s. 257.12(3).

[25] S.O. 1998, c. 33, s. 44, which added s. 257.12.2 to the *Education Act*.

[26] Section 257.12.2(6).

[27] Section 257.12.2(3).

[28] Section 257.12.2(4).

[29] Section 257.12.2(5).

[30] S.O. 1998, c. 3.

municipality to be raised by levying tax rates on business property, other than the roadways and rights of way of railway companies and the transmission corridors of utility companies. The requisition must specify an amount to be raised on each of the following:

(a) the commercial classes;[31]
(b) the industrial classes;[32] and
(c) the pipeline property class prescribed under the *Assessment Act*.

The municipality must then pass a by-law for the levying of the rates specified. The rates must be set by the by-law so that, when levied on the applicable assessment,

(i)   the amount that the requisition requires to be raised on the commercial classes is raised from the commercial classes;
(ii)   the amount that the requisition requires to be raised on the industrial classes is raised from the industrial classes; and
(iii) the amount that the requisition requires to be raised on the pipeline property class is raised from the pipeline property class.

There must be a single rate for each class of real property prescribed under the *Assessment Act*. If there are two or more commercial classes, the rates for the commercial classes must be in the same proportion to each other as the tax ratios established under s. 363 of the *Municipal Act* for the classes are to each other. If there are two or more industrial classes, the rates for the industrial classes must be in the same proportion to each other as the tax ratios established under s. 363 of the *Municipal Act* for the classes are to each other.

The tax rates specified in the by-law passed for the levying of rates are deemed to be tax rates prescribed by the Minister of Finance under the authority granted to him or her to do so by regulation.[33]

The result of these amendments is that the Minister of Finance can requisition amounts to be raised for school purposes from each class of business property instead of prescribing a tax rate or rates. The municipality has to levy the appropriate tax rate on the assessment base to raise the necessary revenues. In either case, the amount collected from business taxes for school purposes will be the same.

Within any given area served by school boards, revenues from the levying of taxes for school purposes on business property are shared on the basis of enrolment. The Ministry of Education and Training calculates and delivers to

---

[31] As determined under s. 363(20) of the *Municipal Act*.
[32] As determined under s. 363(20) of the *Municipal Act*.
[33] *I.e.*, made under s. 257.12(1), (6) of the *Education Act*.

municipalities the "enrolment shares" they are to use to distribute business tax rate revenues to the appropriate district school boards. For example, in a municipality in which there are four coterminous district school boards (English public, English separate, French public, French separate), and the total enrolment of students is divided equally among the four boards, each board would receive 25% of the business tax revenues raised for school purposes.

A municipality with a high business property assessment base ("a rich assessment base") will raise and distribute more revenue per pupil than a municipality with a low business property assessment base per pupil ("a poor assessment base"). The variations in per pupil funding arising from these differences will be equalized by provincial grants.

DISTRIBUTION OF BUSINESS PROPERTY TAXES

A municipality or board that is required to levy tax rates for school purposes on business property distributes the amounts levied in accordance with the following:

1. Where the property is located in the area of jurisdiction of only one board, the amount levied on the property is distributed to that board.
2. Where the property is located in the area of jurisdiction of more than one board, the amount is distributed among the boards in proportion to enrolment in the area as determined and calculated by the Minister.

The Minister determines enrolment and calculates the proportions for each year for each common jurisdictional area and must publish the proportions in the *Ontario Gazette.*[34]

PAYMENT AND COLLECTION OF TAXES[35]

Every municipality must in each year levy and collect the taxes prescribed for school purposes on residential property and business property in the municipality, taxable for school purposes, according to the last returned assessment roll.[36] Every English-language public district school board the area of jurisdiction of which includes territory without municipal organization must in each year levy and collect the tax rates prescribed for school purposes on the residential property and business property in that territory taxable for school purposes, according to the last returned assessment roll. Every district school

---

[34] Section 257.8.
[35] Section 257.7.
[36] Section 257.11.

area board the area of jurisdiction of which includes territory without municipal organization must in each year levy and collect the tax rates prescribed for school purposes on the residential property and business property in that territory taxable for school purposes, according to the last returned assessment roll.

The amounts levied and collected are to be paid in instalments:

1. Twenty-five per cent of the amount levied for the previous calendar year is to be paid on or before March 31.
2. Fifty per cent of the amount levied for the current calendar year less the amount of the first instalment is to be paid on or before June 30.
3. Twenty-five per cent of the amount levied for the current calendar year is to be paid on or before September 30.
4. The balance of the amount levied for the current calendar year is to be paid on or before December 15.

Where an instalment or a part of an instalment is not paid on the due date, the municipality or board in default must pay interest at the specified rate to the recipient board from the date of default to the date that the payment is made. Where, with the consent of the recipient board, an instalment or a part of an instalment is paid in advance of the due date, the recipient board must allow the municipality or payer board a discount from the date of payment to the date on which the payment is due, at the specified rate.

A board can, by agreement with a majority of the municipalities in its area of jurisdiction where the municipalities represent at least two-thirds of the assessment taxable for the purposes of the board, vary the number of instalments and their amounts and due dates. The agreement then applies to all municipalities in the area of jurisdiction of the board.

An agreement which does not provide for its termination continues in force from year to year until it is terminated on December 31 in any year by notice given before October 31 in the year by the secretary of the board as authorized by a resolution of the board or by the clerks of a majority of the municipalities in the board's area of jurisdiction where the municipalities represent at least two-thirds of the assessment taxable for the purposes of the board, according to the last returned assessment roll.

The Minister can make regulations relating to instalments, extending the time for paying of instalments and, in conjunction with the provision of interim financing to boards, directing the instalments to be paid to the province.[37]

---

[37] Section 257.11(12), added by 1998, c. 3, s. 41(1).

TAX REBATES FOR CHARITIES[38]

Every municipality other than a lower-tier municipality must have a tax rebate program for charities for the purpose of giving them relief from taxes on property they occupy. This requirement applies to charities which are registered charities under the *Income Tax Act*[39] with respect to property which is in one of the commercial or industrial classes.

The tax rebate program must provide for a rebate for a charity that pays taxes on property it occupies, except properties for which taxes are capped for 1998, 1999 and 2000. There must be a rebate of at least 40% of the taxes payable by the charity on the property it occupies. If the charity is required to pay an amount under ss. 444.1 or 444.2 of the *Municipal Act*, the amount of the rebate shall be the total of the amounts the charity is required to pay under those sections.

The first instalment of the rebate must be made on or before January 15 of the year and must be for at least half of the estimated rebate for the year. Payment of the balance of the estimated rebate is to be made by June 30 of the year. There must be a rebate even if the charity does not begin to occupy property until after the rebates would otherwise be payable. Final adjustments are to be made in respect of differences between the estimated rebate and the actual rebate to which the charity is entitled. The program must also provide, as a condition of receiving a rebate for a year, that a charity repay any other municipality amounts by which the rebates the charity received for the year from the other municipality exceed the rebates from the other municipality to which the charity is entitled for the year. There must be for a rebate for 1998 and subsequent years.

At the option of the municipality, the tax rebate program may provide for rebates to organizations that are similar to eligible charities or a class of such organizations defined by the municipality. There may be rebates to charities or similar organizations for taxes on property to which Part XXII.1 of the *Municipal Act*, "Capping of Taxes for Certain Property Classes for 1998, 1999 and 2000", applies. There also may be rebates to eligible charities or similar organizations for taxes on property that is not eligible. Rebates also may be greater than those required.

There may be adjustments made in respect of rebates for a year to be deducted from amounts payable in the next year for the next year's rebates. The tax rebate program may also provide for rebates for any year after 1999 (1) to be paid in instalments, each one of which is due 21 days before an instalment of taxes on the property is due, if the percentage that each rebate instalment is

---

[38] These were introduced by amendments to the *Municipal Act* by the *Small Business and Charities Protection Act, 1998*, ss. 27, 28.

[39] R.S.C. 1985, c. 1 (5th Supp.) (as amended to 1998, c. 21).

of the corresponding tax instalment is the same, or (2) to be paid in instalments other than as allowed under (1) if at no time during the year would a charity receive less than it would if the rebate were paid as allowed under (1).

The program may include procedural requirements that must be satisfied for an eligible charity to be entitled to a rebate.

Rebates are given by the municipality unless the municipality is an upper-tier municipality, in which case the rebates are given by the lower-tier municipalities.[40]

Any costs of a rebate of taxes on a property are shared by the municipalities and school boards that share in the revenue from the taxes on the property in the same proportion as the municipalities and school boards share in those revenues. The municipality that gives a rebate to a charity or similar organization shall also give the charity or similar organization a written statement of the proportion of the costs of the rebate that is shared by the school boards.

OTHER TAX REBATES

The council of a municipality, other than a lower-tier municipality, may pass a by-law providing for rebates for owners of all or part of the assessment-related tax increases on properties in the commercial classes or industrial classes. A by-law may require the person who receives a rebate to pay all or part of the rebate to a person who has an interest in the property, including a lessee. ·

The costs of a rebate for a property must be shared by the municipalities and school boards that share in the revenue from the taxes on the property in the same proportion as the municipalities and school boards share in those revenues.

A municipality cannot give a rebate under a program of tax rebates for charities and a rebate under a by-law to the same person in respect of the same property for the same year.

TRANSITIONAL PROVISIONS

Under the *Small Business and Charities Protection Act, 1998* and the *Fairness for Property Taxpayers Act, 1998*, provision has been made to ease the transition from the former system of tax assessment to the new system. These transitional provisions for the capping of taxes and the easing in of tax increases for the years 1998, 1999 and 2000 are provided for in the *Municipal*

---

[40] *Municipal Act*, s. 442.1(6).

Act.[41] The provisions enable the council of a municipality to pass a by-law making the provisions applicable to the three years 1998, 1999 and 2000 in respect of:

(i)   the commercial property class;
(ii) the industrial property class; and
(iii) the multi-residential property class.

If the municipality passes a by-law under Part IIXX.1 or Part XXII.2, Division B, the municipality must maintain frozen assessment listings for the 1998, 1999 and 2000 taxation years, based on the assessment roll for 1997. Changes in the assessments can be made only in accordance with the provisions of the part. The taxes for municipal and school purposes for the three years for a property to which the part is made applicable are determined under the part, not under Division B of Part IX of the *Education Act*. Mill rates for the determination of the amount of taxes are based on 1997 levels, as adjusted in accordance with the part. The taxes are still distributed in accordance with the *Education Act*.

TAXES SET BY BOARDS

Division C of Part IX, "Taxes Set by Boards", is inoperative. Division F of Part IX, "Review of Education Funding", provides that Division C is inoperative with respect to English-language public boards, French-language public district school boards, English-language Roman Catholic boards, French-language separate district school boards and boards of Protestant separate schools.

Cabinet is directed by s. 257.107(1) of the Act to appoint by order a committee "to consider whether the legislation and regulations governing education funding meet the standard set out in subsection 234(2)" of the Act. The order is to specify a date of not earlier than June 20, 2003, when the committee is to commence its work. The committee is to prepare a written report on its deliberations before December 31, 2003. The chair of the committee is to promptly sign the report and submit it to the Minister who in turn is to submit the report to Cabinet and then table the report in the Legislative Assembly. There is no further provision made for what is to then occur.

Nothing may occur.

It is difficult to see what is achieved by Division C and Division F. The presumed intention of Division C is to preserve what may have been thought to

---

[41] See *Municipal Act*, Part XXII.1, "Capping of Taxes for Certain Property Classes for 1998, 1999 and 2000", and Part XXII.2, "Capping of Taxes for Certain Property Classes for 1998/1999 and 2000 — 10/5/5 Percent Cap", Division B, "Optional Scheme for Setting Taxes".

be the minimum constitutional right of separate school boards to raise revenue from their local tax base. It has been used by counsel for the government and separate school trustees to found an argument that, if there is a constitutional right to tax, that right is "suspended" pending a determination of the constitutional validity of Division B. The problems with that position are twofold. First, there is no authority for the proposition that constitutional rights can be "suspended". Secondly, if Division B is held to be constitutional, there can be no constitutional entitlement to the local right to tax contained in Division C. Retaining Division B or reviving Division C would be at the government's option.

Division C is a simplified and reduced version of the provisions relating to local taxation which were in the Act before Bill 160. It provides that for the purpose of raising money for its needs a board may determine, levy and collect rates on assessment for real property that is defined as rateable for the board's purposes.

However, the properties so defined are limited to residential property entered against an individual, partnership or corporation (other than a "designated ratepayer"), and business property entered against an individual or a corporation sole. This excludes all business property assessed against a corporation, public or private (what used to be called commercial and industrial assessment). This approach to local taxation is based on the assumption that, if there was before 1867 a right to tax in separate schools, it was limited to property owned by individuals or partnerships of individuals. This limited view of the protected right to tax is based on the fact that there was no provision in the *Scott Act*[42] for the taxation of corporations and that only individuals could be separate school supporters.

EDUCATION DEVELOPMENT CHARGES[43]

School boards which require new sites for schools because of residential development and insufficient capacity within the schools currently operated by the board may impose education development charges on residential and non-residential land undergoing development for the purposes of site acquisition. The costs to a board which can be recovered through education development charges are "education land costs" only. These are the costs to acquire, service and prepare the land for building, and of pupil accommodation, the interest thereon and the costs of any background studies required to be distributed.

---

[42] S.U.C. 1863 (2nd Sess.), c. 5. The Ontario Court of Appeal has held that school boards have no constitutional right to tax: *Bill 160 Case* (1999), 172 D.L.R. (4th) 193. This decision is under appeal to the Supreme Court of Canada. See also discussion in Chapter 1 under heading "Constitutional Position of Public Boards".

[43] See, generally, Part IX, Division E, of the *Education Act*.

"Pupil accommodation" is any building required to accommodate pupils or an addition or alteration to a building that enables the building to accommodate an increased number of pupils.

The developments upon which a charge may be imposed are those which require a zoning by-law, a minor variance, subdivision approval, consent to severance, approval of a description under the *Condominium Act*[44] or a building permit.

Education development charges are provided for in a by-law passed by the board, which remains in force for a maximum of five years, and which must:

(a) designate the categories of residential development and non-residential development on which an education development charge shall be imposed;

(b) designate those uses of land, buildings or structures on which an education development charge shall be imposed;

(c) designate the areas in which an education development charge shall be imposed; and

(d) subject to the regulations, establish the education development charges to be imposed in respect of the designated categories of residential and non-residential development and the designated uses of land, buildings and structures.

Anyone can appeal a by-law to the Ontario Municipal Board within 40 days of its passing. The board must hold a hearing and can dismiss the appeal in whole or in part, order the board to repeal or amend the by-law, or itself repeal or amend the by-law.

The Ontario Municipal Board has no jurisdiction to increase the amount of an education development charge payable in any particular case, to remove or reduce the scope of an exemption, or to change the date the by-law will expire.

An education development charge is payable upon a building permit issued to the municipality issuing the building permit. A municipality must not issue a building permit for development to which an education development charge applies unless the charge has been paid. A board that has passed an education development charge by-law must establish reserve funds in accordance with the regulations.

An owner or a board may complain to the council of the municipality to which an education development charge is payable that:

(a) the amount of the education development charge was incorrectly determined;

---

[44] R.S.O. 1990, c. C.26 (as amended to 1997, c. 24).

   (b)   a credit is, or is not, available to be used against the education development charge or the amount of the credit was incorrectly determined; or

   (c)   there was an error in the application of the education development
charge by-law.

A complaint must be made not later than 90 days after the day the education
development charge or any part of it is payable.

The council's decision can be appealed to the Ontario Municipal Board
within 40 days of its date. If the council does not deal with the complaint, a
party can appeal within 60 days after the complaint was made. The Ontario
Municipal Board holds a hearing and can dismiss the appeal or rectify any
incorrect determination or error that has been made.

Exemptions, procedure for publicizing and passing the by-law, determination of the charges and amendments to by-laws and the education development
charges reserve fund are dealt with by regulation.[45]

Money from an education development charge reserve fund may be used
only to fund costs that meet all of the following criteria:

1. The costs are education land costs.
2. The costs are growth-related net education capital costs as defined in Part III
   of the *Development Charges Act*,[46] "Education Development Charges", the
   predecessor of Division E of the *Education Act*.
3. The costs are incurred for the purpose of acquiring land or an interest in
   land in the region of the area of jurisdiction of the board in which the real
   property disposed of is located.[47]

A constitutional challenge to education development charges was rejected
by the Supreme Court of Canada[48] on the ground that, although they constitute
indirect taxes,[49] they are ancillary to a valid comprehensive and integrated
regulatory scheme for the provision of educational facilities as a component of
land-use planning. The Court also held that the charges did not prejudicially
affect the rights of separate school supporters. The charges are not "rates" but a
new source of funds. The scheme of charges is integrated with the funding
model of the *Education Act* and treats public and separate schools equally.

---

[45] *Education Development Charges — General*, O. Reg. 20/98 (as amended to O. Reg. 473/98).

[46] R.S.O. 1990, c. D.9 (renamed *Education Development Charges Act*, 1997, c. 27, s. 69(1)).

[47] O. Reg. 20/98.

[48] *Ontario Home Builders' Assn. v. York Region Board of Education* (1996), 137 D.L.R. (4Th) 449 (S.C.C.).

[49] Under s. 92(1) of the *Constitution Act, 1867*, a province may impose only "direct taxes", *i.e.*, taxes paid by the person taxed, not passed on to the ultimate consumer, in this case the home buyer.

11

New Funding Model: Provincial Grants

LEGISLATIVE GRANTS REGULATIONS

Provincial grants are contained in the annual legislative grants regulations made by Cabinet under the power in the Act to "make regulations governing the making of grants for educational purposes from money appropriated by the Legislature".[1] The regulations may:

(a) provide for the method of calculating or determining any thing for the purposes of calculating or paying all or part of a legislative grant;

(b) prescribe the conditions governing the calculations or payment of all or part of a legislative grant, including a condition that the approval or confirmation of the Minister is required for anything prescribed by the regulation;

(c) authorize the Minister to withhold all or part of a legislative grant if a condition of the legislative grant is not satisfied; or

(d) require that all or part of a legislative grant be repaid if a condition of the grant is not satisfied.

The regulations are subject to two important statutory requirements. First, they must ensure that the legislation and regulations governing "education funding" operate in a fair and non-discriminatory manner, in particular, with respect to English-language public boards and English-language Roman Catholic boards, and French-language public district school boards and French-language separate district school boards.[2] Secondly, the regulations must ensure that the legislation and regulations governing education funding operate so as to respect

---

[1] *Education Act*, s. 234. The regulation for 1998-99 has a new name: see now *Student Focused Funding — Legislative Grants for the School Board 1998-99 Fiscal Year*, O. Reg. 287/98 (as amended to O. Reg. 212/99).

[2] *Education Act*, s. 234(2). For "education funding", see discussion, *infra*, at p. 136.

the rights provided for in s. 23 of the *Canadian Charter of Rights and Freedoms.*[3]

The first of these requirements is a comparative one. The operation of the funding must be fair and non-discriminatory when a comparison is made between the two types of English-language boards. Similarly, the operation of the funding must be fair and non-discriminatory when a comparison is made between the two types of French-language boards. The "fair and non-discriminatory" principle has no application in a comparison of the two types of public boards or the two types of separate boards.

The second requirement is not a comparative one. The funding of French-language boards must fulfill the obligations of the province to francophones under s. 23 of the Charter, as interpreted and explained by the courts.

The reason for the distinction lies in the different nature of the constitutional protections, for denomination on the one hand and minority language on the other. The rights of separate schools were defined prior to Confederation in relation to the rights and powers of common schools with respect to both powers of local taxation and entitlement to provincial grants. Minority-language rights, on the other hand, are defined in absolute, not comparative, terms.

"Education funding" in this context means revenue available to a board:

(a) from provincial grants;
(b) from tax rates under Part IX, Division B, of the Act, other than tax rates for the purpose of paying rebates; and
(c) from taxes under Part XXII.1 of the *Municipal Act,*[4] or Division B, "Optional Scheme for Setting Taxes", of Part XXII.2 of the *Municipal Act*, other than taxes for the purposes of paying a board's share of the costs of rebates or paying rebates;[5] and
(d) from education development charges under Division E of Part IX of the *Education Act.*

Cabinet may also make regulations providing for funding to assist a board in adapting to the education governance and education funding reforms of 1997 and 1998. These regulations cannot be made for the purpose of assisting a board after August 31, 2001. In special circumstances, a regulation may be made in respect of a board or boards until August 31, 2003.

As the provincial grants are contained in the annual regulations, their structure may theoretically be changed from year to year, subject only to fulfilling the mandates in the Act. However, the general legislative grants regulations made prior to Bill 160 had been in substantially the same form for many years.

---

[3] Section 234(3).
[4] R.S.O. 1990, c. M.45 (as amended to 1998, c. 33).
[5] *Education Act*, s. 234(13).

Further, the grant structure contained in the first regulation made under Bill 160 reflects the funding model which the government had long worked on, which reflected its philosophical approach. It was published in March, 1998, accompanied by a number of technical and background studies and the reports of four expert panels. It can be assumed that the new grant structure has at least intended permanence.[6]

Under the new (student-focused) funding model, a district school board is paid a grant, the amount of which is determined as follows:

1. Determine the 1999-2000 tax revenue of the board.[7]
2. Determine the amount of each type of allocation for the board.[8]
3. Total the amounts determined for the board in step 2.
4. Adjust the amount determined in step 3 to take into account phase-in funding.[9]
5. Add the stable funding guarantee amount, if any, determined for the board.[10]
6. Deduct the amount determined for the board in step 1 from the amount determined for the board in step 5.
7. Deduct fees revenue received by the board under the 1999-2000 fees regulation.[11]
8. Deduct the amount that is in the board's reserve fund, resulting from a strike or lock-out, on August 31, 2000, immediately before its transfer into general revenue.[12]
9. Add the total of the amounts payable to the board for capital projects.[13]

The new "student-focused" funding model replaces the former 34 categories of grants with the following allocations:

   (i) the foundation allocation, and
  (ii) special purpose allocations for:

---

[6] See *Student Focused Funding — Legislative Grants for the School Board 1998-99 Fiscal Year*, O. Reg. 287/98 (as amended to O. Reg. 212/99); *Student Focused Funding — Legislative Grants for the School Board 1999-2000 Fiscal Year*, O. Reg. 214/99.

[7] Determined in accordance with the complex formula in O. Reg. 214/99, s. 12.

[8] See grant allocations in O. Reg. 214/99, ss. 13-34.

[9] O. Reg. 214/99, s. 40. See discussion under heading "Phase-in Funding", *infra*.

[10] O. Reg. 214/99, s. 48. See discussion under heading "Stable Funding Guarantee", *infra*.

[11] See *Calculation of Fees for Pupils for the 1999-2000 School Board Fiscal Year*, O. Reg. 215/99.

[12] Reserve fund provided for in s. 233(1) of the Act, transferred under s. 233(2).

[13] O. Reg. 214/99, s. 49. See Chapter 12, "Capital Funding".

- special education
- language
- small schools
- remote and rural
- learning opportunity
- summer school remedial allocation
- adult education, continuing education and summer school
- teacher compensation
- retirement gratuities[14]
- early learning
- transportation
- administration and governance
- debt charges
- pupil accommodation

In addition, the grants regulation provides for:

- phase-in funding
- stable funding guarantee
- grants to isolate boards
- grants to s. 68 boards
- payments to governing authorities
- enveloping
- grants for certain capital projects

FOUNDATION GRANTS

The foundation grant to a board covers the basic costs of providing an educational program for one school year and is allocated to school boards on a per pupil basis. The amount of the foundation grant for each pupil is the same regardless of where a board is located in Ontario.

The foundation grant for a secondary school student is higher than the foundation grant for an elementary student, to recognize the higher costs of providing secondary education. For the year 1999-2000, it is $3,953 for a secondary student, $3,367 for an elementary student.

The foundation grant is comprised of ten components which constitute the cost elements of education common to all boards for pupils in Ontario. It covers the following costs.

---

[14] Added to O. Reg. 287/98 by O. Reg. 537/98 but not contained in O. Reg. 214/99.

1. *Classroom Teachers*: salaries and benefits for certified classroom teachers, supply teachers and occasional teachers, and professional development for teachers.
2. *Teacher Assistants*: salaries and benefits for staff who support certified teachers.
3. *Textbooks and Learning Materials*: textbooks, workbooks, equipment, computer software, library books and resource materials.
4. *Classroom Supplies*: other classroom supplies, including paper, pens and pencils, art materials and classroom equipment.
5. *Classroom Computers*: computer hardware and network costs.
6. *Library and Guidance Services*: salaries and benefits for school librarians and guidance counsellors.
7. *Professional and Paraprofessional Support*: salaries and benefits for staff providing support services to students and teachers (includes psychologists, psychometrists, speech therapists, social workers, community workers, child/youth workers, attendance counsellors, library and computer technicians, recreational staff, pastoral agents (*e.g.*, chaplains and animateurs culturelles)).
8. *Preparation Time*: salaries and benefits for additional teachers to enable teachers to spend time for lesson preparation, pupil assessment consultation with other teachers and meetings with parents and students.
9. *Teacher Consultants*: salaries and benefits for teacher consultants and co-ordinators who provide teachers with advice about programs and student needs (includes reading specialists, science specialists, specialists in conflict resolution and specialists in assisting teachers with implementing the provincial curriculum).
10. *School Administration*: salaries and benefits for principals, vice-principals, department heads and school secretaries, and the costs of school office supplies.

The foundation grant does not cover the additional costs associated with students' special needs, the circumstances of particular schools or boards, or the provision of programs. Neither does it cover the costs of administration, transportation or pupil accommodation. These are covered by other grants.

The new funding model contains a number of formulae incorporating values and coefficients which affect the actual level of funding to which a school is entitled. To identify appropriate benchmarks, Ministry officials analyzed school board expenditures in the ten categories and calculated a range of standard measures, such as averages and adjusted averages (weighted and unweighted), medians and means. The distribution of expenditure patterns in these categories was also assessed using common statistical procedures.

Medians were, on balance, the preferred statistical measure of school board expenditures in most categories. This measure reflects the level of expenditures where half the school boards spend more and half spend less in a particular category.

The selection of benchmarks reflected government policy. Important benchmarks such as the funding for classroom teachers reflected the limit on average class size set by Bill 160. The funding for preparation time at the secondary level reflected the minimum teaching time set by Bill 160.

Specific program mandates imposed on school boards were also reflected. Statistically generated benchmarks in areas such as guidance services were supplemented to recognize the additional requirement for these services in the secondary school reforms beginning in 1998-99.

The purchasing power of benchmark amounts was also evaluated. The allocation in the foundation grant for textbooks for elementary students is $75 per student per year. This benchmark reflects information provided by the Ministry's curriculum branch, obtained through meetings with textbook publishers, which established that an average textbook costs $25 to $35 and is in use on average for 5 to 7 years. The Ministry's approach has been criticized on the basis that it does not meet the real needs or costs of boards across the province.

An amount of $50,000 a year was used as a benchmark for teacher salaries to arrive at an "average salary grid". However, the actual teachers' salary grids of many boards, which reflect the real costs, are higher than the national "average salary grid".

Similar criticisms have been directed at other elements of the foundation grant: the allocations per pupil for classroom supplies, computers and textbooks were based on system-wide expenditures. On this basis, the amount allocated for each elementary pupil for computers was set at $43. However, the Ministry staff made no analysis of perceived adequacy of expenditures in this area. No attempt was made to determine the number or educational usefulness of the computers presently owned by boards. Rather, all boards, irrespective of their needs and irrespective of their existing computer resources, were allocated $43 for each elementary pupil.

SPECIAL PURPOSE GRANTS

Special purpose grants are made to boards to cover the additional costs of meeting special needs of students, addressing the particular circumstances of schools and boards, and offering certain programs. They also provide funding for board expenditures not covered by other grants, including transportation, adult and continuing education, administration and governance.

Special Education Grants

The special education grant funds the additional costs of students with special needs. It has two components:

1. *Special Education Per Pupil Amount* (SEPPA): This allocation covers the costs of providing additional assistance to the majority of students with special needs. It is based on total enrolment and is allocated to boards on a per pupil basis.
2. *Intensive Support Amount* (ISA): This allocation covers the needs of particular students who require individualized high-cost assistance. ISA funding is based on the enrolment of individual students who meet the criteria for ISA funding; the funding follows the student in a move to another board.

Although ISA funding is related to individual pupils with unusually high-cost special education needs, SEPPA funding is based on a board's total enrolment, irrespective of the incidence of non-ISA special education needs within the board. The amounts for 1999-2000 are $362 for each elementary student enrolled and $229 for each secondary student enrolled.

This approach to funding special education needs has been criticized as being unfair as between English-language public boards and English-language Roman Catholic boards. Public boards usually serve a proportionately higher number of students with special education needs than Roman Catholic boards. The Toronto District School Board is particularly disadvantaged, as it serves a proportionately higher number of students with special education needs compared to other boards, both public and Roman Catholic. The former Metropolitan Toronto public boards spent approximately $335 million annually for special education, of which approximately $200 million reflected additional support costs above the average amount required to educate non-exceptional students. The new funding model provides approximately half this amount to the Toronto District School Board for 1998 to 2001.

Provision is made by regulation requiring boards to establish a special education reserve fund,[15] where the amount spent by a board on special education in a fiscal year is less than a prescribed amount. The amount to be deposited into this reserve account is the amount of expenditure for special education (other than for "programs in facilities") which is *less* than A-B where:

A is the allocation for special education under the legislative grants legislation.
B is the amount for special education "programs in facilities" determined by the school board under the legislative grants regulation.

---

[15] *Reserve Funds*, O. Reg. 446/98, s. 4.

"Programs in facilities" are the education programs that are considered in determining the programs in facilities amount for the board under the legislative grants regulations. "Facilities" are institutions other than schools, such as hospitals, nursing homes and places of detention.

Language Grants

The language grant supports programs to help students learn the language of their classroom or a second language. It is made up of five components:

1. *French as a First Language*: funds French-language boards for the higher instructional, materials and administrative costs required for French-language education. The grant is based on the number of pupils enrolled.
2. *French as a Second Language*: funds English-language boards for the additional costs of providing core French, extended French and French immersion programs. The grant is based on the number of students enrolled in these programs and the average daily length of the program. At the elementary level, funding for French immersion covers Junior Kindergarten to Grade 8. Funding for core and extended French covers Grade 4 to Grade 8.
3. *Native as a Second Language*: funds boards providing instruction in Aboriginal languages. The grant is based on the number of students enrolled in the program and the average daily length of the program.
4. *English as a Second Language* (ESL) *and English Skills Development* (ESD): funds English-language school boards which provide language instruction in regular day school programs for students whose first language is not English. The amount of the grant is based on the number of students under 21 actually enrolled in the board's schools who have immigrated to Canada within the past three years from a country where "standard" English is not the first language.
5. *Actualisation Linguistique en Français* (ALF) *and Perfectionnement du Français* (PDF): funds French-language school boards that provide language instruction for students who, although entitled to attend, have limited competency in French. The allocation is based on two components:
   (i) a component which provides funding for additional teachers based on enrolment in the board and an "assimilation factor" which measures the percentage of students in the French language board relative to the total students, English and French, within the same geographic area of the board; and
   (ii) a component which provides funding based on the number of immigrant students who entered Canada during the last three years from countries where French is a language of administration or schooling and who need to familiarize themselves or increase their competency in the language of instruction.

Small Schools Grants

Funding is provided to recognize the additional costs of operating small schools. Small elementary schools are defined as those having less than an average of 20 pupils per grade and located eight or more kilometres from other elementary schools within defined boundaries. Small secondary schools are defined as having less than an average of 120 pupils per grade and located 32 or more kilometres from other secondary schools within defined boundaries. Funding for such schools is provided on a sliding scale based on the number of students per grade (the "small size factor") and the distance between schools with the board (the "remoteness factor").

Remote and Rural Grants

This grant funds the additional costs of operating boards in rural areas with sparse pupil populations. Funding is based upon a "per pupil distance amount" and a "per pupil sparsity amount" derived from the "pupil density" (A.D.E.[16] divided by the board's area in square kilometres).

Learning Opportunity Grants

Learning opportunity grants support a range of programs, to be identified by the board, designed to help students who are at greater risk of academic failure because of social and economic factors. The amount of the grant is based on four demographic factors, assumed to result in students at a high risk of failure. The funding model provides "an interim approach for the 1998/99 school year", based on 1991 census information. The four factors are:

   (i)   low income;
   (ii)   low education of persons 15 years or over;
   (iii)   recent immigration; and
   (iv)   aboriginal origin.

Where the population in an enumeration area is at least twice the 1991 provincial norm in respect of any one of the four factors, that area will qualify for a portion of the total learning opportunity grant for the province, which was set at $185 million in 1998-99. However, an eligible area's amount of that funding will be based solely upon the area/province comparison in respect of low income, whether or not it exceeds the provincial norm. Only students 17 years of age or younger will qualify for consideration, despite the fact that many regular secondary school students are over this age.

---

[16] A.D.E. means the "average daily enrolment" as determined under O. Reg. 213/99, *Calculation of Average Daily Enrolment for the 1999-2000 Fiscal Year.*

Where an area qualifies for a learning opportunity grant, the amount for the area is divided among the four types of boards who have jurisdiction over the area (English-public, English-Roman Catholic, French-public, French-Roman Catholic), according to school-aged population, irrespective of the relative incidence of the four factors within the various school boards.

The legislative grant regulation for 1998-99 allocates an amount for this grant to every board in the province, ranging from $152,434 for the Bruce-Grey Catholic board to $53,334,398 for the Toronto public board. Although the amounts presumably reflect the calculated share of the "area grant", the regulation does not demonstrate that the amounts of the total provincial grant of $185 million were calculated by reference either to actual identified needs or the cost of adequately serving those needs. There is no evidence that these apparently arbitrary numbers will be sufficient to meet the needs of the high-risk learners served by the boards throughout the province.

Summer School Remedial Allocation

This grant is for summer school classes and courses. A "summer school class or course" is a class or course provided by a board between the hours of 8 a.m. and 5 p.m. which starts after the completion of the 1999-2000 school year and ends before the start of the 2000-2001 school year for developmentally delayed pupils, or one in which a pupil may earn a credit or a credit equivalent.

Only pupils who were enrolled in a day school program offered by a board in the 1999-2000 school year are counted for the purposes of this grant. The amount of the grant for the 1999-2000 fiscal year is the average daily enrolment multiplied by $2,257, plus an amount for transportation costs related to the remedial instruction.

Adult, Continuing Education and Summer School Grants

These are grants to boards to fund education for adults 21 and over for credit courses leading to an Ontario Secondary School Diploma and non-credit second language training in English or French. They also provide for high school students pursuing credit courses in summer school, and for elementary school students studying international languages outside of their normal instructional day.

The amount of the grant for 1998-99 is essentially based upon the pre-1998 grant level, that is, $2,257 per average daily enrolment. There is, however, no evidence to establish that this per pupil amount is, on average, sufficient to meet the educational needs of adult learners across the province.

The $2,257 figure does not appear to be based upon any analysis of the cost of educating adult learners. Rather, it can be traced to a dispute between the Metropolitan Toronto School Board and the province in the mid-1980s involving the education by that board of adult Roman Catholic Separate School supporters.

At the time, the cost for grant purposes of continuing education was recognized by the province as being the same as the cost for adolescent day school (approximately $4,000 per student). However, the province paid only a portion of continuing education costs according to a formula which was based inversely on a board's assessment wealth. In the case of Metropolitan Toronto, funding for continuing education students was only approximately 10% of the $4,000. The shortfall was made up by public school ratepayers in Metropolitan Toronto.

Because of the broad scope of the adult programs offered by the Toronto boards of education, they attracted considerable numbers of separate school supporters. Based on the opinion of learned counsel, the Toronto public boards told the Minister that it could be obliged by law either to refuse separate school supporters or charge them a fee.

In order to resolve the issue, the board and the province agreed that the cost of continuing education was less than that of regular day school and the province would pay 100% of a "continuing education" cost to be fixed by agreement. This amount was fixed at 50% of the regular day school amount without any analysis as to its adequacy. This resulted in a figure of approximately $2,000, which over the years became the amount of $2,257 "continued" by the legislative grant regulation.

The former metropolitan area boards spent significantly more per adult learner than the $2,000 amount negotiated in the mid-1980s. This was in part due to the high number of recent adult immigrants who required assistance in languages. These boards also educated a very large number of adult students who were unsuccessful in secondary education while they were younger and who required special learning supports and a day school environment in order to succeed.

There is at present no provision for adult learners who are at the same time "special needs" learners. Because they are older than 17 years of age, these learners do not qualify for "learning opportunity" funding. Funding them at the arbitrary level of $2,257 will disadvantage them compared to other adult learners.

Teacher Compensation Grants

Teacher compensation grants provide funding to school boards to recognize the variation in salary costs related to the qualifications and experience of its teachers. The grant is in addition to the funding for teacher salaries provided through the foundation grant.

Teachers are compensated according to a "grid" negotiated between school boards and teacher federations which relates salaries for teachers to years of experience and academic qualifications. Under this grant, boards identify the placement of their teachers on an average salary grid. Funding is based on the weighting of teachers on this grid. Boards with a higher percentage of senior teachers would receive more funding.

In 1999-2000, this grant includes two components which provide additional funding to school boards. The first component is provided to recognize that school boards have to implement new instructional time standards at the secondary level which came into effect on September 1, 1998, and will require funding to effect this transition. The second component provides funding to school boards whose average credit load for secondary students exceeds 7.2; funding will be provided to a maximum average of 7.5 credits.

Retirement Gratuity Grants

These grants provided money for retirement gratuities for "eligible retirees" who were defined as persons who ceased, voluntarily, to be employed by a district school board at the end of the 1997-98 school year and who were eligible to receive an immediate pension under the *Teachers' Pension Act*:[17]

(i)   teachers who were members of a teachers' bargaining unit, but not occasional teachers or continuing education teachers; and

(ii)   principals and vice-principals, other than those in respect of whom the board was eligible to receive a transition assistance grant under the applicable guideline.

The "retirement gratuity" covered was a sick leave gratuity or other lump sum allowance payable by a board in accordance with a collective agreement or board policy in effect on April 1, 1998, but not an amount payable under an early retirement incentive plan of the board. The amount of the grant was calculated in accordance with the amending regulation.[18] The grant was payable only in the fiscal year 1998-99.

Early Learning Grants

Many school boards offer Junior Kindergarten programs to four-year-old students. These programs are funded through the foundation grant, special purpose grants and the pupil accommodation grant.

Where a school board does not offer Junior Kindergarten, money is provided to the board through an early learning grant to use in enriching its programs for Senior Kindergarten to Grade 3 or providing other program and educational supports for early learners.

---

[17] R.S.O. 1990, c. T.1.

[18] Added to O. Reg. 287/98 by O. Reg. 537/98 but not contained in O. Reg. 214/99.

Boards which offer Junior Kindergarten in some schools but not in others receive funding for their Junior Kindergarten enrolment as well as receiving early learning grants.

Transportations Grants

Transportation grants fund certain costs of transporting students to and from school and from school to school, including the transportation of special needs students.

For 1998-99, each school board's funding for transportation was based upon 97% of its 1997 expenditures (as disclosed by the "costing framework").[19] This amount in subsequent years will be adjusted up or down (or will stay at 97% of 1997 expenditures) in accordance with the growth or decline of the board's total enrolment. This reduction to 97% of the 1997 expenditures occurred despite the fact that boards are obliged by Bill 160 to operate their schools for an additional five days compared to the 1996-97 and 1997-98 school years. This reflects a further expansion of service need by 2.5%.

Boards which elect to receive the early learning grant to offer Junior Kindergarten for the first time receive nothing under the transportation grant for the increased need for transportation services.

Administration and Governance Grants

These grants provide the money to pay for the administration and governance of boards. They cover:

(i) an amount for board members' honoraria and expenses and for expenses relating to pupil representation;
(ii) an amount for directors of education and supervisory officers; and
(iii) an amount for administration costs.

The grant amounts for each of these areas of expense is set out precisely in the regulation. A board receives $5,000 for the honorarium, $5,000 for the expenses of each trustee, $10,000 for additional honoraria for the chair and vice-chair, and $5,000 for expenses relating to pupil representation.

The amount for directors of education and supervisory officers is determined as follows:

---

[19] The "costing framework" was a new approach used by the Working Group on Education Finance Reform to survey expenditure patterns of school boards. The working group was set up by the Minister of Education and Training in March, 1995, and consisted of representatives of school boards and teachers' federations.

1. Allow $200,000 as a base amount (increased from $65,000 in the previous year).
2. Allow $23 per pupil for the first 25,000 pupils of the board (in the previous year $67 for the first 2,000 and $25 for the next 23,000).
3. Allow $21 per pupil for the remaining pupils of the board.
4. Total the amounts allowed in steps 1 to 4.
5. Add 2% of the amount of the board's remote and rural allocation.[20]
6. Add 0.5% of the amount of the board's learning opportunities allocation.[21]
7. Add 1% of the amount calculated for the board for new pupil places.

The amount for the board for administration costs is determined as follows:

1. Allow $80,000 as a base amount.
2. Add the product of $174 and the 1999-2000 day school average daily enrolment of pupils of the board.
3. Add 11% of the amount of the board's remote and rural allocation.
4. Add 0.5% of the amount of the board's learning opportunities allocation.
5. Add 1% of the amount calculated for the board for new pupil places.

Debt Charges Grants and Pupil Accommodation Grants

The purpose of the debt charges grant is to provide money to service debt incurred in the acquisition of certain capital assets. The pupil accommodation grant provides for the operation and renewal of schools as well as for the provision of new pupil places. These grants are discussed in detail in Chapter 12, "Capital Funding".

Miscellaneous Funding

Phase-in Funding

The purpose of the provisions in the regulation with respect to phase-in funding is to make adjustments to the amount of the provincial grant based on changes in operating revenue from the previous year. The change in operating revenue is arrived at by dividing the operating revenue for the 1999-2000 fiscal year for the board by the operating revenue for the 1998-99 fiscal year for the board. Account is then taken of changes in enrolment to arrive at the adjusted change in operating revenue. If the resulting change is more than 1.04 or less than 0.96, calculations are made to determine the amount to be added or subtracted, as the case may be, to the grant for each board.

---

[20] As determined under s. 30 of O. Reg. 214/99.
[21] As determined under s. 31 of O. Reg. 214/99.

Stable Funding Guarantee

This guarantee was introduced in the grants regulation for 1999-2000. The stable funding guarantee amount for a district school board is the amount by which the operating revenue for the 1998-99 fiscal year for the board exceeds the amount determined for the board as its operating revenue for 1999-2000, plus the approved special incidence ISA claims for pupils of the board.

Grants to Isolate Boards

An isolate board is a school authority other than a s. 68 board.[22] The approved expenditure of an isolate board is the expenditure that is acceptable to the Minister as shown on the forms provided by the Ministry to the isolate board for the purpose of calculating the 1999-2000 legislative grant.

In determining the approved expenditures for isolate boards, the Minister applies the funding formula for grants to district school boards "with such adaptations as the Minister considers advisable to take account of characteristics particular to school authorities".[23]

Grants to Section 68 Boards

A s. 68 board is composed of members appointed by the Minister to exercise school board powers over schools on lands held by the Crown and other lands exempt from school taxes. A s. 68 board is paid a grant based on its expenditure for the 1998-99 fiscal year that is acceptable to the Minister for grant purposes, excluding:

    (i)   expenditures for debt charges;

    (ii) expenditures for the purchase of capital assets;

    (iii) expenditures for the restoration of destroyed or damaged capital assets; and

    (iv) provisions for reserves for working funds and provisions for reserve funds,

minus

    (i)   any transfers from reserves for working funds or from reserve funds made during the 1998-99 fiscal year;

    (ii) revenue of the board from sources other than,

---

[22] For "school authority", see discussion in Chapter 4 under heading "Terminology". For "s. 68 boards", see "Grants to Section 68 Boards", *infra*.

[23] O. Reg. 214/99, s. 55(2).

    (a) legislative grants;

    (b) an organization on whose property a school of the board is located; and

    (c) refunds of expenditure of the kind described above.

Payments to Governing Authorities[24]

Provision is made for payments to be made under agreements between the Minister and the governing authorities of Crown establishments. A "Crown establishment" is an establishment maintained by a department of the Government of Canada, a federal Crown company, the Royal Canadian Mounted Police or Atomic Energy of Canada Ltd. on Crown lands that are not assessable for school purposes, and Indian reserves. The agreements provide for payment for the education of pupils resident in a territorial district or on a Crown establishment who attend a school supported by local taxation in Manitoba or Quebec and pupils resident in a territorial district who attend a school on a reserve.

Enveloping

Prior to the 1998-99 legislative grant regulation, the only conditions imposed on the boards' spending of provincial grants were:

1. The legislative grants payable to a board for elementary school purposes had to be applied to elementary school purposes and the legislative grants payable to a board for secondary school purposes had to be applied to secondary school purposes.
2. If a board failed to comply with the Acts administered by the Minister, the regulations and the policy and program initiatives, the Minister could withhold all or part of a legislative grant payable until the board took corrective action.
3. Where the amount payable to a board under a previous regulation was either overpaid or underpaid, the overpayment or underpayment was deducted from or added to the legislative grant.
4. Where a board was convicted of an offence or was held by a court to have contravened an Act, the Minister could exclude from grant assistance any money spent by the board for legal fees, fines and damage awards imposed as a result.

It is now a condition of the payment of a grant to a district school board that the board manage its estimates process and its expenditures so as to ensure compliance with a list of stringent requirements. District school boards must ensure that net classroom expenditure amounts are at least equal to their 1999-

---

[24] See O. Reg. 214/99, Part IV.

2000 classroom expenditure allocation amount. There are detailed provisions for the calculation of the classroom expenditure allocation and the classroom expenditure amount.

A district school board also must ensure that an amount equal to the total of the special education allocation and the amount placed in the board's special education reserve fund in the fiscal year September 1, 1998, to August 31, 1999, less the programs in facilities amount determined for the board, is spent in the 1999-20000 fiscal year on special education for pupils of the board. Where the board's expenditure on special education for 1999-20000 is less than the net special education allocation and the amount in the reserve fund for 1998-1999, the board must place the difference in the board's special education reserve fund.

A board must ensure that the amount of the allocations for school renewal and for new pupil places is spent on the acquisition of capital assets. If the board's expenditure on the acquisition of capital assets is less than those allocations, the board must place the difference in the board's pupil accommodation reserve fund.

It is a condition of the payment of all grants to a district school board that the board manage its estimates process and expenditures so that the total of its administration expenditures and governance expenditures does not exceed the allocation therefor. If there is a cost overrun, the board must submit a written plan to the Minister or update its previous plan, outlining how it proposes to reduce its administration and governance expenditures so that, by the fiscal year 2000-2001, spending does not exceed its allocation.

The categorization of classroom and non-classroom expenditures are governed by the Ministry's 1998-99 "Uniform Code of Accounts".

MUNICIPAL GRANTS

All grants, investments and allotments made by a municipality or by a local board of a municipality for education purposes must be shared with the boards whose area of jurisdiction is all or partly the same as the area of jurisdiction of the municipality or the local board, on the basis of enrolment.

12

Capital Funding

FORMER CAPITAL FUNDING MODEL

Under the old capital funding model in effect before Bill 160, boards of education had both the responsibility to meet as well as a degree of control over their capital needs. They raised the money necessary for capital projects either by local taxation or, for projects approved by the province, by a combination of local taxation and provincial grants. The cost of a capital project which was paid from local taxes was known as the "local share". Boards could construct projects not approved by the province entirely from the local share with no provincial grant being provided. They were also free to build approved projects the cost of which exceeded the approved capital cost. The unapproved cost could be funded from the local share.

Revenues raised through local taxation could be applied towards capital projects in the current year or used to repay outstanding debentures issued to finance capital expenditures in prior years. The total amount which could be debentured by a public board was controlled by regulation. If a board's debt service limit exceeded the prescribed amount, the approval of the Ontario Municipal Board (OMB) was required. The regulation did not apply to Roman Catholic separate school boards.

The province contributed capital grants for the construction of new facilities and additions and for the repair and renovation of existing facilities but only for a project or part of a project approved by the Minister. The criteria for approval were contained in the "Capital Grant Plan, 1979". The amount of the grant was the prescribed share of the lesser of the actual cost and the cost approved by the Minister. Each year, the general legislative grants regulation listed all boards in the province and prescribed a particular share for each board which would determine the part of the cost of a board's capital projects to be paid by the province in the form of a capital grant.

Capital grants were calculated so that, for a given amount of approved expenditure per pupil, all boards would make the same tax effort. Boards with a richer assessment base per pupil would pay a larger portion of the approved cost from the local share.

A board that wished to lease facilities had to justify the need for additional facilities by completing a "Co-operative Study of Need". The Ministry's approval was sought through regional offices and had to be accompanied by a copy of the lease agreement. If the lease extended beyond the term of the trustees of the board, it was subject to OMB approval. Grants were based on the appropriate pupil accommodation charge, the number of pupils and the length of the lease.

The capital approval process required provincial intervention at a number of stages. This required significant effort towards compliance on the part of boards and extensive supervision by the Ministry. The allocation process was seen by school board officials as both inconsistent and subjective. They expressed the need for a process of determining capital requirements that would be rational and easily understood and which could be applied consistently across the province.

Boards were required to stand in line for provincial approvals for capital grants. The total amount of spending was set and limited by the province. As the province was funding its share of the approved cost of the projects as they were incurred, this imposed limits on the projects which could be approved. Boards also frequently encountered problems with the timing of approvals, which limited a board's ability to plan for the construction of new schools as enrolment increased.

As boards could finance capital projects from their local tax revenues, boards with a richer assessment base per pupil were better able to do so than boards with a poorer assessment base. The richer boards could augment the approved costs of a capital project and add other features, such as auditoriums and extra-large gymnasiums, to their schools.

The criticisms directed at the former model for funding board operations and programs applied equally to the process for the funding of capital needs.

NEW CAPITAL FUNDING MODEL

The principal changes in capital funding brought about by the new model are that the province determines the amount of funding available to boards and the purposes for which they can be spent but within the framework boards determine their own priorities without having to obtain Ministry approval.

The province provides to each board a pupil accommodation grant for three distinct purposes: new pupil places; school renewal; and school operations. Each component of the grant is exclusively dedicated to its particular purpose.

The grant for new pupil places and the grant for school renewal must be deposited by a board in its Pupil Accommodation Reserve Fund and used exclusively for these purposes.[1] Money in the fund not used in the fiscal year stays there for use in future years for the dedicated purposes.

The dedication of these allocations, that facilities are maintained in good repair and new facilities provided as enrolment grows, ensures that funds are available for capital purposes when needed. Processes for the construction and major maintenance of schools often stretch over many years beyond the electoral mandate of a single board. The requirement to "envelope" these funds and separate them from annual budgets and expenditure enables a long-term planning approach.

Within the envelope, boards are free to determine their own priorities. The grants may be used to finance new school construction, meet debenture payments for new capital projects, enter into long or short-term lease arrangements for premises, enter into multi-use partnership agreements with other boards, municipalities and the private sector, or provide temporary accommodation for students in areas where enrolment is expected to decline. The priorities can be met without the need to wait their turn at the Ministry's counting-house or navigate the complex system of Ministry approvals.

The province will monitor the impact, economy and effectiveness of the new model. To ensure continuing accountability, the Expert Panel on Pupil Accommodation recommended that boards submit every three years a long-range plan for new schools and facilities renewal based on enrolment projections, provide an annual report on the use of funds for school operation and renewal, and provide reports on major projects, so that the relative efficiency and effectiveness of project design, construction, business practice and financing can be assessed.

PUPIL ACCOMMODATION GRANTS[2]

The pupil accommodation grant to a board consists of amounts for:

(i)   school operations;
(ii)   school renewal; and
(iii)   new pupil places.

The amount of the grant is calculated using separate formulae to determine allocations for school operation (heating, lighting, cleaning and maintenance), school renewal (repairs and renovations), and new pupil places, which reflect the factors influencing need.

---

[1]   See *Reserve Funds*, O. Reg. 446/98.
[2]   See also Chapter 11 under heading "Legislative Grants Regulations".

The grants are determined on a per pupil basis. The formulae used to calculate grant allocations for individual boards distinguish between the traditional elementary and secondary school panels and adult education. The basic structure of the formula is the same for each category, specifically:

Grant for New Pupil Places	Enrolment in excess of Capacity	x	Benchmark Area Requriement per Pupil	x	Benchmark Construction Cost per sq. ft.	x	Geographic Adjustment Factor	
Grant for School Renewal	Enrolment	x	Benchmark Area Requirement per Pupil	x	Benchmark Renewal Cost per sq. ft			
Grant for School Operation	Enrolment	x	Benchmark Area Requirement per Pupil	x	Benchmark Operating Cost per sq. ft.			

School Operations

The grant for school operations is the total of:

(i)   the elementary school area requirement (A.D.E.[3] X 9.29 m^2); plus

(ii) the adult education, continuing education and summer school area requirement (A.D.E. of pupils over 21, pupils in day school credit courses and summer school A.D.E. x 9.29 m^2); plus

(iii) the secondary school area requirement (A.D.E. x 12.07 m^2),

all multiplied by $55.97.

The Minister must approve a supplementary elementary school area factor and a supplementary secondary school area factor for a board if the Minister considers that it is appropriate to do so in order to make allowance for disproportionate space needs that are particular to the board and that are caused by:

(a) the fact that the board is reasonably operating a school that is too large for the community it serves;

(b) the fact that the board is reasonably operating a school in a building the physical characteristics of which are neither compatible with nor easily modified to conform to the benchmark area requirements;

(c) the fact that the board has higher space requirements because the board serves a high number of pupils in special education programs or in other education programs with high space requirements;

(d) other similar circumstances.

---

[3] A.D.E. means the "average daily enrolment" as determined under O. Reg. 213/99, *Calculation of Average Daily Enrolment for the 1999-2000 Fiscal Year.*

The school area requirements are then adjusted to reflect the factor applied. In the 1999-2000 regulation, the supplementary school area factors are also required to be used to calculate a top-up amount for each elementary school and secondary school.

School Renewal

The grant amounts for boards for school renewal are based on "weighted average benchmarks" for school renewal costs per square metre. These benchmarks are arrived at by allocating $6.89 for each square metre of total school area less than 20 years old and $10.33 for each square metre of space more than 20 years old. The weighted average benchmark is the total of these two amounts.

The amount of the grant is the board's school area requirement multiplied by the weighted average benchmark and, for 1999-2000, a top-up amount which takes into account the capacity of each school in terms of pupil places.

New Pupil Places

The grant amounts for new pupil places are based on the A.D.E. minus school capacity of pupil places as determined by the Minister. If the result is a positive number, the grant is this number multiplied by the benchmark area requirement, in turn multiplied by the benchmark construction costs. These benchmarks are 9.29 m^2 and $118.40 per square metre for elementary capacity, and 12.07 m^2 and $129.17 per square metre for secondary capacity.

"Pupil places" for these purposes consist solely of "instructional space", that is, space that can "reasonably" be used for instructional purposes. Using school facilities data, the Minister identifies categories of instructional space. In identifying categories of instructional space, the Minister has regard to but is not limited to the categories identified by the Pupil Accommodation Review Committee in their report of August, 1998. The Minister then assigns a loading to each category of instructional space so identified, based on the number of pupils that can reasonably be accommodated in each category of instructional space. To determine school capacity, the Minister applies the loadings to the instructional spaces as categorized.

The Minister can make adjustments to take into account funds received by one board from another board in connection with a determination made under the regulation respecting the disposition of an asset of an old board.[4]

"School facilities data" is the data relating to boards' school facilities, including school floor plans and other data compiled in accordance with the Ministry's school facilities inventory system.

---

[4] *Transition from Old Boards to District School Boards*, O. Reg. 460/97 (as amended to O. Reg. 477/98).

The amount of the grant for 1999-2000 is the lessor of $20 million and the amount determined in accordance with the methods summarized here.

CAPITAL PROJECTS GRANTS

Provision was made in the legislative grants regulation for 1998-99 for the payment of grants for capital projects where:

(a) the Minister gave an approval in writing of the estimated cost for the project on or before September 1, 1998; and

(b) the Minister gave final approval in writing for the project during the period beginning September 1, 1998, and ending August 31, 1999.

The legislative grants regulation for 1999-2000 provides that a grant or portion of a grant that was payable to a district school board under a previous legislative grants regulation in respect of any capital project, other than a capital project under the Canada-Ontario Infrastructure Works,[5] and that is not paid before September 1, 1999, is not payable under the regulation or under any previous legislative grants regulation. Any grant or portion of a grant that was payable to a district school board under a previous legislative grants regulation in respect of a Canada-Ontario Infrastructure Works capital project and that is not paid before September 1, 1999, is deemed to be a grant payable under the 1999-2000 regulation.

DEBT CHARGES GRANTS

The amount of the debt charges allocation for a district school board is the total of the payments on account of principal and interest due and payable by the board in the fiscal year in order to service debt incurred by the board or a predecessor old board of the board to finance the acquisition of a capital asset where:

(a) the acquisition is pursuant to a contractual obligation entered into by the board or predecessor old board before May 15, 1998; or

(b) the acquisition is for the purposes of a capital project the estimated project cost of which was approved in writing by the Minister before May 15, 1998.

---

[5] A Canada-Ontario Infrastructure Works capital project is a project funded under the Canada-Ontario Infrastructure Program Agreement, dated January 1, 1994, and amended August 26, 1996.

With respect to debt incurred before May 15, 1998, the grant is not payable if the amount, terms or conditions of the obligation have been renegotiated, unless the renegotiated amount, terms and conditions are approved in writing by the Minister. The grant is payable in respect of debt incurred after May 15, 1998, only if the amount, terms and conditions of the debt are approved in writing by the Minister.

RESERVE FUNDS

The regulation governing reserve funds requires the establishment of the following reserve funds.

Pupil Accommodation Allocation Reserve Fund[6]

Every school board must allocate the pupil accommodation allocations received under the legislative grants regulation for school renewal and new pupil places (but not for allocations for school operations) to a reserve fund established only for the purpose of acquiring by purchase, lease or otherwise,

(a) school sites with school buildings on them;
(b) school buildings, fixtures of school buildings and additions, alterations, renovations or major repairs to school buildings or fixtures;
(c) furniture or equipment to be used in school buildings;
(d) library materials for the initial equipping of libraries in school buildings; and
(e) water supplies and electrical power supplies on school properties or the means of conveying water or electrical power to school properties from outside the properties.

Special Education Reserve Fund

An amount must be deposited into this reserve fund if the amount of a board's expenditure for special education (other than for programs in facilities) is *less* than: the allocation for special education under the legislative grants regulation *minus* the amount for special education programs in facilities determined for the board under the legislative grants regulation. "Programs in facilities" are the education programs that are considered in determining the programs in facilities amount for the board under the legislative grants regulations. "Facilities" are institutions other than schools, such as hospitals, nursing homes and places of detention.

---

[6] Provided for in *Reserve Funds*, O. Reg. 446/98.

Education Development Charges Reserve Fund

These reserve funds are for the proceeds of a disposition of property which was acquired with funds withdrawn from an education development charges account or education development reserve fund, where the property was not used to provide school accommodation. The net proceeds of such a disposition must be allocated to the education development charges account established under the education development charges by-law or to the education development charges reserve fund established under the regulation.[7]

Reserve Fund Following Strike or Lock-Out

If in any fiscal year money provided in the estimates of a board for payment of salaries and wages of teachers and other employees in relation to employment in that year is not paid because of a strike or lock-out of the teachers and other employees, that money must be put in a reserve. The amount in the reserve at the end of the fiscal year must be brought into the general revenues of the board for that fiscal year.

The regulation presently in force provides for the amount that a board must put in this reserve fund. The amount is arrived at by subtracting amounts in the fiscal year which are approved by the Minister as necessarily and reasonably incurred by the board as a result of the strike or lock-out from the total of the salaries, wages and benefits,

   (i)   that are in effect on the day that the strike or lock-out commences;

  (ii)   that are included in the estimates of the board in the fiscal year; and

 (iii)   that are not payable, or are payable but reimbursable, to or in respect of employees of the board for the period of a strike by or lock-out of those employees, or any such class of them, that occurs in the fiscal year.

DISPOSITION OF SCHOOL BOARD PROPERTIES

Although school boards may have revenues which are not covered by the funding model, such revenues are for the most part in payment for additional services provided.[8] A more lucrative source of income for school boards would seem to be from the lease, sale or other disposition of property which a board no longer needs.[9] These transactions and their proceeds are, however, subject to

---

[7] See *Education Development Charges — General*, O. Reg. 20/98 (as amended to O. Reg. 473/98).

[8] Examples of revenues not covered include: tuition fees from foreign students and Native students; revenues from governments for providing training or programs; interest income on capital or other reserves; investments; and donations.

[9] See *Disposition of Surplus Real Property*, O. Reg. 444/98 (as amended to O. Reg. 57/99), which revoked and replaced *Disposition of School Sites*, O. Reg. 497/98.

restrictions. Under the *Education Act*, a school board may sell, lease or dispose of a school site or *any property* of the board if it adopts a resolution:

(a) that the site or part of the site or property is not required for the purposes of the board; or

(b) that the sale, lease or other disposition is a reasonable step in a plan to provide accommodation for pupils on the site or part of the site or property.

Proposals for Disposition

If a board proceeds to dispose of the property, it must issue a proposal to its coterminous boards, any colleges within its jurisdiction, the university nearest to the property, the municipality, the local services board, the provincial government and the federal government. The municipality or the province may refer the proposal to any of its "local boards", not including a school board. The province may also refer the proposal to any provincial agency, board or commission. The federal government may refer the proposal to any federal agency, board or commission. A board may, but is not obliged to, include the Ontario Realty Corporation in its proposal.

There is a limited class of transactions to which the proposal and offer process does not apply. The school board may dispose of a property *at fair market value* to a municipality or a local board of the municipality if the purpose of the acquisition is to provide one or more of the municipal hard services listed in the *Education Development Charges Act.*[10]

A "local board" is a public utility commission, transportation commission, public library board, park management board, local board of health, police services board, planning board or other body established or exercising power in the municipality, but does not include:

(a) a neighbourhood committee or community council;

(b) a children's aid society or conservation authority; or

(c) a school board.

These dispositions are not subject to the proposal process.

Acceptance of Offer

An institution contemplating an offer in response to a proposal does not have to justify its need for the property. If an offer is made, the board may only accept an offer which complies with the regulation and which is made by the body having the highest priority on the list in the regulation.

---

[10] R.S.O. 1990, c. D.9 (Act title rep. & sub. 1997, c. 27, s. 69(1)).

If offers are made by two or more bodies that have the same priority (*e.g.*, two provincial agencies), priorities among them are determined by the board.

Acquisition Price

The general principle is that acquisitions be at fair market value. However, this is subject to important exceptions with respect to proposals made for:

   (i)   the sale of schools;
  (ii) the sale of schools to the Ontario Realty Corporation; and
 (iii) the sale of a school to be used as a school by the purchaser.

Proposals for Sales of Schools

A proposal for the sale of a school may provide for a sale at no cost. An offer may be made by another school board, and only by another school board (subject to the next paragraph), in response to a proposal for purchase at no cost.

A proposal for the sale of a school to the Ontario Realty Corporation may also provide for a sale at no cost to the corporation. An offer may be made by the corporation in response to such a proposal, for purchase at no cost. The Ontario Realty Corporation has a lower ranking on the priority list for the acceptance offers than the coterminous school boards but a higher ranking than all other institutions.

Meaning of "School"

The provisions of the regulation of specific application to schools apply to all properties on which there is a building that is used "for providing pupil accommodation" (*i.e.*, as a school). The provisions also apply to properties on which there is a building that was last used as a school as well as to properties on which there is a building that was last used as a school even if since last used as a school it was used "by the board" primarily for storage or maintenance purposes.

Offers for School to be Used as School

Offers for schools must, in specified cases, be the *lesser* of:

  (i)   fair market value; and
 (ii) for elementary schools, capacity x 9.29 m^2 x \$1,259 per square metre (sale) or \$129.17 per square metre (lease),

or

 (ii) for secondary schools, capacity x \$1,356 per square metre (sale) or \$129.17 per square metre (lease).

These requirements apply in the case of a school where the body making the offer to acquire is a coterminous board or where the purpose of the body making the offer is to acquire the property in order to use the building to accommodate pupils for use by the Ontario School for the Deaf or for an education program that under the legislative grants regulations would be considered in determining a board's "programs in facilities" amount.

Acquisition of School by Another Board

There are special provisions applicable where a school has been acquired or leased by another school board at less than market value.

Sale

If a board enters into an agreement for sale of a school in response to a proposal, the agreement must provide that, if the purchasing board does not use the site or part of the site to provide accommodation for pupils eligible to be included in the calculation of legislative grants for new pupil places for any period of 12 consecutive months within the 25 years after the sale or the commencement of the lease, the purchasing board must offer the site or part of the site for sale to the school board at the price which the purchasing board paid, within the time specified in the agreement.

Lease

If the board enters into an agreement for lease of a school in response to a proposal, the agreement for lease must provide that, if the leasing board does not use the site or part of the site to provide accommodation for pupils eligible to be included in the calculation of legislative grants for new pupil places for any period of 12 consecutive months within the 25 years after the sale or the commencement of the lease, the lease terminates.

Sale of Properties Other Than Schools

There are special provisions in the reserve funds regulation[11] on the acquisition of administration buildings. A board may use moneys in the Proceeds of Disposition Reserve Funds to acquire real property to be used by the board for board administration purposes and additions, alterations, renovations or major repairs thereto. However, the amount which a board can use for this purpose cannot exceed the net proceeds of dispositions of the buildings used for administration purposes by the old board immediately before January 1, 1998. All proposals for the disposition of administration buildings and other properties not used as schools must be at fair market value.

---

[11] O. Reg. 446/98.

Determination of Fair Market Value

The following procedure must be followed with respect to a proposal for sale or lease at fair market value. If there is disagreement on "fair market value", the board and the offeror may:

(a) negotiate for 30 days, and agree on a price; or
(b) where they cannot agree, the board may withdraw its offer or have the price determined by binding arbitration.

If no price is agreed to at the termination of the 30-day period or the body withdraws its offer or does not elect binding arbitration, the board may consider instead the offer made by the body that has the next highest priority and whose offer complies with the regulation.

Proceeds of Disposition Reserve Fund (PDRF)[12]

Every school board must allocate all proceeds of dispositions of real property to a reserve fund established only for the purpose of acquiring, by purchase, lease or otherwise:

(i) school sites that provide or are capable of providing pupil accommodation and any additions or improvements to such school sites;
(ii) school buildings or fixtures of school buildings, and additions, alterations, renovations or major repairs to school buildings or fixtures of school buildings;
(iii) furniture and equipment to be used in school buildings;
(iv) library materials for the initial equipping of libraries in school buildings; and
(v) water supplies or electrical power supplies on school properties or the means of conveying water or electrical power to school properties from outside the properties.

The requirement applies to the proceeds of:

(i) any leases entered into before January 1, 1998; and
(ii) renewals after January 1, 1998, of leases entered into before that date.

A school board must also allocate to the PDRF all proceeds of property insurance on the properties, regardless of whether the property was acquired with money from the PDRF. The moneys in the PDRF may be used, in defined circumstances, for the acquisition of administration buildings.

---

[12] Provided for in O. Reg. 446/98.

The following moneys do not have to be allocated to the PDRF:

(a) proceeds that are required to be allocated to an education development charges account or the Education Development Charges Reserve Fund;

(b) proceeds that the board is required to pay to another board under an agreement approved by the Education Improvement Commission; or

(c) proceeds that the board is required to pay to the federal government under an agreement under s. 188(3) of the Act.[13]

---

[13] Section 188(3) enables a school board to enter into an agreement with the federal government to provide for a payment from the Crown to provide additional classroom accommodation and tuition for Indian pupils. It says nothing about payments by a board to the Crown.

13

Finances of Boards

BOARD ESTIMATES[1]

Before Bill 160, every board was required to prepare and adopt estimates of the moneys required during the year for public school and secondary school purposes. Each board then submitted to the council of the municipality on or before the first day of March in each year a statement indicating the amount of the estimates for school purposes to be raised by the council and a requisition of the amount required to be raised by the council for education purposes. Each board determined its own budget and the council was obliged to levy the amount requisitioned by the board.

A board still has to prepare and adopt estimates each year but the estimates now are of "the revenues and expenditures for the fiscal year". They are to be adopted by a date specified by the Minister and it is mandatory that they:

(a) set out the estimated revenues and expenditures of the board, including debt charges payable by the board or on its behalf, ensuring that the latter do not exceed the former;
(b) provide for a projection of any surplus or deficit arising in the preceding fiscal year;
(c) make allowance for a surplus from any previous fiscal year that will be available during the current fiscal year, including a projected surplus;
(d) provide for any deficit of any previous fiscal year, including a projected deficit;
(e) not provide for any future deficit; and
(f) provide for the mandatory allocations to reserve funds.

The main changes effected by Bill 160 are that a board must now provide for any projected deficit as well as a known deficit from the preceding year, or

---

[1] See *Education Act*, Part IX, Division A, ss. 231-233.

any surplus, and the power to provide for a reserve fund for permanent improvements is replaced by detailed requirements established by regulation. The Minister can issue guidelines for the form and content of estimates and require boards to comply with the guidelines and submit a copy of the estimates to the Ministry by a specified date.

In its discretion, a board can provide for a reserve for working funds of not more than 5% of its expenditures for the preceding fiscal year. The total in this reserve fund cannot exceed 20% of its expenditures for the preceding fiscal year.[2]

There are provisions with respect to reserve funds for permanent improvements and the Minister is given the power to make regulations with respect to these funds. Under the existing regulation, the maximum amount that a school board can allocate from its revenues to a reserve fund for permanent improvements in a fiscal year is determined by adding to 1% of the revenue fund revenues for the board for the fiscal year, the estimated revenue from the sale or disposal of or from insurance proceeds in respect of permanent improvements.[3]

A reserve fund must also be established for money that was provided in the estimates of a board for payment of salaries and wages of teachers and other employees in a year which was not paid out because of a strike by or lock-out of the teachers or other employees. The amount in the reserve at the end of the fiscal year must be brought into the general revenues of the board for that fiscal year. The regulation presently in force provides that the amount that a board must put in this reserve fund is arrived at by calculating the total of the salaries, wages and benefits,

(a) that are in effect on the day the strike or lock-out commences;
(b) that are included in the estimates of the board in the fiscal year; and
(c) that are not payable or are payable but reimbursable to or in respect of employees of the board for the period of a strike by or lock-out of the employees or any such class of them that occurs in the fiscal year.[4]

Any amounts in the fiscal year which are approved by the Minister as necessarily and reasonably incurred by the board as a result of the strike or lock-out are subtracted from the calculated total.

---

[2] See Section 231(1) of the Act and *Reserve for Working Funds Limit*, O. Reg. 496/97.
[3] See *Reserve Funds*, O. Reg. 446/98.
[4] *Calculation of Amount of Reserve Resulting from Strike or Lock-out*, O. Reg. 486/98.

FINANCIAL ADMINISTRATION OF BOARDS

The "financial administration" of boards is not to be confused with "supervision of boards' financial affairs" by the Minister in the event of a board having financial difficulties. The financial administration of boards is carried out by the boards themselves and their auditors.

The requirements of the Act relate to boards' financial statements and the duties of the auditor of a board. It is the obligation of the treasurer of a board to:

(a) prepare the financial statements for the board by the date prescribed by the Minister;

(b) upon receipt of the auditor's report on the financial statement, promptly give the Ministry two copies of the financial statements and the auditor's report;

(c) within one month after receiving the auditor's report on the board's financial statements,

    (i) publish the financial statements and the auditor's report in a daily or weekly newspaper that in the opinion of the treasurer has sufficient circulation within the area of jurisdiction of the board to provide reasonable notice to those affected by them,

    (ii) mail or deliver a copy of the financial statements and auditor's report to each of the board's supporters, and

    (iii) otherwise make the information in the financial statements and auditor's report available to the public to the extent and in the manner directed by the Minister.

The board's auditor who is appointed by the board has the following rights:

(a) to have access at all reasonable hours to all records of the board and to require from the members and officers of the board any information and explanation that in the auditor's opinion may be necessary to enable the auditor to carry out his or her duties;

(b) to require any person to give evidence on oath or affirmation for the purposes of the audit and, for the purposes of the testimony, the auditor has the powers of a commission under Part II of the *Public Inquiries Act*,[5] which applies as if the auditor were conducting an inquiry under that Act; and

(c) to attend any meeting of the board or of a committee of the board, to receive all notices relating to that meeting that a member is entitled to

---

[5] R.S.O. 1990, c. P.41.

receive, and to be heard at the meeting that the auditor attends on any part of the business of the meeting that concerns him or her as auditor.

A member or officer of a board who refuses or neglects to provide access to the records of the board or information or an explanation required by the auditor is guilty of an offence and on conviction is liable to a fine of not more than $200. However, there can be no conviction if the accused proves that he or she made reasonable efforts to provide the access or the information or explanation.

BORROWING BY BOARDS AND DEBT LIMITS[6]

Long-Term Borrowing

All long-term borrowing by a board must be by way of debenture issued pursuant to a by-law passed by the board and must:

(a) be for the purpose of "permanent improvements";

(b) be within the limits of debt and financing liability limits of the board; and

(c) comply with the relevant provisions of:
  (i) the *Education Act;*
  (ii) the regulations made under the Act; and
  (iii) the provisions of the *Municipal Act* made applicable to boards by the regulation.[7]

Cabinet has the power by regulation to prescribe instruments other than debentures that a board can issue for money borrowed but has not yet done so.

A board may also by by-law borrow for permanent improvements by loan from a bank, a trust company or a credit union within the meaning of the *Credit Unions and Caisses Populaires Act, 1994,*[8] with an initial maturity of more than one year. The board must ensure that the proceeds of the loan are used only for permanent improvements.

---

[6] The provisions with respect to borrowing and debentures are contained in: *Education Act*, ss. 241, 243-249; *Borrowing for Permanent Improvements: Issuance of Debentures*, O. Reg. 466/97; and the sections of the *Municipal Act* which by s. 4 of the regulation are made applicable to money by-laws passed and debentures issued by school boards. The limits imposed on the debt and other financial obligations of school boards are governed by s. 242 of the *Education Act* and the regulations made under the section: *Debt and Financial Obligation Limits*, O. Reg. 472/98; and *Current Borrowing Limits*, O. Reg. 495/97.

[7] See *Borrowing for Permanent Improvements: Issuance of Debentures*, O. Reg. 466/97.

[8] S.O. 1990, c. 11 (as amended to 1997, c. 28).

A school authority may by by-law borrow money or incur debt for permanent improvements and issue debentures therefor, with the prior approval of the Minister.

"Permanent Improvements"

The Act contains a definition of "permanent improvement" but the definition is not exhaustive.[9] It is defined to include:

   (a) a school site and any additions or improvements to a school site;

   (b) a building used for instructional purposes and any additions, alterations or improvements to a building used for instructional purposes;

   (c) any additions, alterations or improvements to an administration building;

   (d) a teacher's residence, a caretaker's residence, a storage building for equipment supplies and any additions, alterations or improvements to such a residence or storage building;

   (e) furniture, furnishings, library books, instructional equipment and apparatus, and equipment required for maintenance of the property described in (a) to (d) and (f);

   (f) a bus or other vehicle, including watercraft, for the transportation of pupils;

   (g) the obtaining of a water supply or an electrical power supply on a school property or the conveying of a water supply or an electrical power supply to a school from outside the school property;

   (h) initial payments or contributions for past service pensions to a pension plan for officers and other employees of the board; and

   (i) any property, work, undertaking or matter prescribed by the Minister in a regulation.

Bill 160 made some changes to the definition. An "administrative office" is no longer a permanent improvement but only additions, alterations or improvements to an "administration building". A child care facility is no longer a permanent improvement.

The Minister's power to extend the definition of permanent improvement is entirely new. There has also been one change made to the definition of "school site" which is now "land or premises . . . required by a board for a school, school playground, school garden, teacher's residence, caretaker's residence, gymnasium, school offices [rather than, as before, 'offices'], parking area or for any other school purpose".

---

[9] *Education Act*, s. 1(1).

Mandatory Provisions of Borrowing By-Laws

While there are a number of permissive provisions governing the content of borrowing by-laws, some provisions are mandatory. A money by-law must provide that the whole debt and any debentures to be issued for it shall be made payable within a term not to exceed the lifetime of the undertaking, up to a maximum of 40 years. A money by-law for the issuing of debentures must provide for:

(a) repayment of the principal in annual instalments; and
(b) payment of interest on the unpaid balance in one or more instalments each year.

A by-law must require the board to provide for payment of the principal and interest payable on the debentures issued under the by-law as follows:

1. The board must provide in its estimates for each fiscal year for the setting aside out of its general revenue in the fiscal year the amount necessary to pay the principal and interest coming due on the debenture in the fiscal year and the amount required to be paid into a sinking fund or retirement fund.
2. On or before each due date in each year, the board must pay out of its general revenue the principal and interest coming due on the debenture or debt instrument in the year.

The principal and interest that must be paid in a year does not include any outstanding amount of principal specified as payable on the maturity date of a debenture if the debenture has been refinanced.

By-Laws for Sinking Fund Debentures

A money by-law for the issuing of sinking fund debentures must provide for the setting aside in each year of the currency of the debentures and for payment from general revenue of:

(a) an amount sufficient to pay the interest payable on the debentures in that year; and
(b) a specified amount for the sinking fund that, with interest at a rate of not more than 8% per annum compounded yearly, will be sufficient to pay the principal of the debentures at maturity.

The principal and interest payable under refinancing debentures must be raised in the same fashion as for the original debentures.

The treasurer of a board which is obligated to set aside amounts for a sinking fund must prepare and lay before the board every year before the board adopts the estimates a statement showing what amount will be required for that purpose.

By-Laws for Term Debentures

A money by-law for the issuing of term debentures must provide for:

(a) the setting aside in each year of the currency of the debentures of an amount sufficient to pay the interest payable on the debentures; and
(b) the setting aside in each year of the currency of the debentures in which no other debentures issued under the same by-law become due and payable of a specified amount to form a retirement fund for the debentures that, with interest at a rate not to exceed 8% per annum compounded yearly, will be sufficient to pay the principal of the debentures at maturity.

The by-law must provide that the amounts payable shall be set aside and paid by the board out of general revenue.

By-Laws for Extendible Debentures

A by-law passed with respect to extendible or retractable term debentures must provide for the setting aside in each year of the currency of the debentures of:

(a) an amount sufficient to pay the interest payable on the debentures in that year; and
(b) a specified amount to form a retirement fund.

The specified amount for the retirement fund must be equal to or greater than the amount that would have been required to have been set aside and paid in each year in respect of the principal amount of the debentures if:

(a) the principal had been payable in equal annual instalments; and
(b) the board had issued the debentures for the maximum period that it authorized by by-law for the repayment of the debt for which it issued the debentures, commencing on the date of the debentures.

The by-law must provide that the amounts payable shall be set aside and paid by the board out of general revenue.

The period for which an extendible term debenture may be extended must expire within the maximum period of years that was authorized by the by-law of the board for the repayment of debentures issued for the debt for which the extendible debenture was issued, commencing on the date of the extendible debenture.

A by-law passed with respect to extendible term debentures must:

(a)   fix the rate of interest during the initial term; and
(b)   provide that the rate of interest payable for any extended term,
   (i)   shall be the same as the original amount fixed,
   (ii) shall be such different rate as is set out in the by-law, or
   (iii) shall be a rate determined by a further by-law passed not less than six months prior to the maturity date.

Permissive Provisions for Borrowing By-Laws

A money by-law may provide that all or part of the debentures shall be redeemable at the option of the board on any date prior to maturity, subject to the following provisions:

1. The by-law and every debenture that is so redeemable shall specify the place of payment and the amount at which the debenture may be so redeemed.
2. The principal of every debenture that is redeemable shall become due and payable on the date set for the redemption and from and after such date interest ceases to accrue where provision is made for the payment of the amount.
3. Notice of intention to redeem must be sent by post at least 30 days prior to the date set for redemption to the person in whose name the debenture is registered at the address shown in the debenture registry book.
4. At least 30 days prior to the date set for redemption, notice of intention to redeem must be published in the *Ontario Gazette* and in a newspaper of general circulation, if any, in the municipality and in such other manner as the by-law may provide.
5. If only part of an issue of debentures is to be redeemed, the part shall comprise only the debentures with the latest maturity dates. No debenture issued under the by-law shall be called for redemption in priority to a debenture issued under the by-law with a later maturity date.

A board may provide in a money by-law that all or a portion of a debenture to be issued is a term debenture payable on a fixed date with interest payable in one or more instalments in each year. The retirement fund for a term debenture must be administered in all respects in the same manner as a sinking fund and the provisions of the *Municipal Act* with respect to a sinking fund apply, with necessary modifications, to the retirement fund.

If a by-law authorizes sinking fund debentures to be issued, the by-law may authorize the issuing of debentures to refund at maturity the outstanding sinking fund debentures. The refunding debentures shall be payable within the maximum period of years that was authorized by the municipality for the repayment of the debt for which debentures were issued, commencing on the date the original debentures were issued.

A money by-law may provide that all or a portion of the debentures are sinking fund debentures which have the principal payable on a fixed date and interest payable in one or more instalments in each year.

Extendible and Retractable Debentures

A board can provide in a money by-law that all or part of the debentures to be issued shall be payable at a fixed date, with interest payable in one or more instalments in each year, but the board must:

(a) extend the term of all or any of the debentures at the request of the holder given to the treasurer at any times fixed in the by-law before the maturity date of the debentures and subject to any conditions that may be set out in the by-law; or

(b) if the debentures have a maturity date longer than five years, redeem all or any of the debentures at the request of the holder at earlier dates than fixed in the by-law subject to any conditions that may be set out in the by-law.

By-Laws to Refund Debentures

If property acquired with proceeds of the sale of debentures is sold while any part of the debentures remains outstanding, the net proceeds of the sale must be applied towards the amount of principal and interest then outstanding on the debentures. A by-law can be passed providing for the issue of debentures to refund at maturity existing debentures still outstanding. The refunding debenture must be payable within the maximum period of years that the board originally authorized by by-law for the repayment of the debt for which it issued debentures.

Consolidating By-Laws

Where separate debenture by-laws have been passed authorizing borrowing for two or more purposes, instead of borrowing the separate amounts authorized to be borrowed and issuing debentures therefor, the board can by by-law (a consolidating by-law) provide for borrowing the total amounts and for issuing one series of debentures. The consolidating by-law must clearly specify, by recital or otherwise, the separate by-laws which it consolidates.

A consolidating by-law may authorize the issue of debentures in one series even if some of the debentures may be for different terms from the other debentures to be issued thereunder. The amount to be raised in each year under the consolidating by-law must equal the total amount that would have been raised under the separate by-laws. The debentures issued under a consolidating by-law need not refer to the separate by-laws which have been consolidated.

Repealing By-Laws

A repealing by-law must recite the facts on which it is founded and must be expressed to take effect on August 31 in the fiscal year of its passing. Where only part of a sum of money provided for by a by-law has been raised, a board may repeal the by-law as to any part of the remainder and as to a proportionate part of amounts to be raised annually.

Debentures Generally

A by-law for the issuing of debentures can provide for issuing them on any date specified in the by-law or in sets in the amounts and on the dates required. The board may by by-law extend the date for an issue of debentures or sets of them.

All the debentures must be issued within two years after the passing of the by-law unless the proposed expenditure for which the by-law provides is estimated or intended to extend over a number of years and it is undesirable to have large amounts of the money in hand unused and uninvested. In that case, if the board believes it would not be of advantage to so issue them, the by-law can provide that the debentures may be issued in amounts and at times as the circumstances require. The first of the sets must nevertheless be issued within two years and all of them within five years after the passing of the by-law.

The board can by by-law authorize a change in the mode of issue of the debentures. The by-law can provide that the debentures be issued with coupons instead of in amounts of combined principal and interest, or vice versa. Where debentures have been sold, pledged or hypothecated by the board, upon again acquiring them or at the request of any holder of them, the board can cancel them and issue one or more debentures in substitution for them. Debentures issued in substitution can be made payable by the same or a different mode on the instalment plan but no change can be made in the amount payable in each year.

The last instalment of an instalment debenture must mature no earlier than five years after the date of its issue. The debenture must specify the principal amount payable under the debenture in the final year that the board must raise by issuing refunding debentures.

A debenture may be registered as to principal and interest, in which case the interest must paid by cheque or, if authorized in writing by the owner of the debenture, by electronic transfer. The debenture may be referred to as a fully registered debenture.

The following records may be kept electronically or by using a magnetic medium:

(a) copies of certificates of ownership and original memoranda of debenture transfers;

(b) names and addresses of the owners of registered debentures; and

(c) particulars of the cancellation and destruction of debentures and the issuance of any debentures in exchange.

Any writing produced from an electronic or magnetic medium that represents the copy of a certificate of ownership kept in a readily understandable form is admissible in evidence to the same extent as a copy of the certificate. If there is no original written record, any writing produced from an electronic or magnetic medium that is in a readily understandable form and that represents a memorandum of debenture transfer or the records is admissible in evidence to the same extent as if it were an original written record.

A debenture may be made payable to bearer or to a named person or bearer.

The full amount of a debenture is recoverable even if it was negotiated at a discount by the corporation.

A debenture must bear the seal of the board and the signatures of the head of the board, or another person authorized to sign by a by-law of the board, and the treasurer. The seal and signatures may be printed, lithographed, engraved or otherwise mechanically reproduced. Interest coupons, each bearing the treasurer's signature, may be attached to a debenture. A debenture and interest coupons are sufficiently signed if they bear the required signatures and each person signing has authority to do so on the date of signing.

Debentures may bear any date or dates specified in the issuing by-law, including a date before the by-law is passed, if the by-law provides for the first levy being made in the year in which the debentures are dated or in the next year. Every debenture in a set or issue of debentures must bear the same date.

Guarantees by Province

Cabinet can authorize the Minister of Finance to guarantee payment by the province of the principal, interest and premium of debentures or debt instruments issued by a board. The authorization may relate to a single debenture or instrument or to a class of debentures or instruments as such class is defined in the authorizing order in council.

The form of the guarantee and the manner of its execution shall be determined by order of the Cabinet and every guarantee executed in accordance with the order is conclusive evidence of the guarantee. A debenture guaranteed by the province is valid and binding on the board which issued it, according to its terms.

Proceeds of Sale/Pledge of Debentures

With certain specific exceptions, proceeds of the sale or pledge of debentures must be:

(a) kept in a separate account;

(b) used only for the purposes for which the board issued the debentures; and

(c) not applied towards payment of the current or other expenditures of the board.

The exceptions apply in situations where a board has more money on hand from the sale of debentures than it needs.

There are three possible eventualities. First, if the proceeds of the sale of debentures are not required immediately for the purpose for which the board issued the debentures, the board may invest the money in the general fund of the board. The board must in that case ensure two things. It must credit to the debenture account interest on the money invested and it must return to the debenture account by August 31 the amount of principal and interest on the debentures payable or payable into the sinking fund or retirement fund in the following year. However, if money received from the sale or pledge of debentures is not required for the purposes for which the debentures were issued, it may be applied to buy back the debentures or to meet any other capital expenditure of the board. If property acquired with all or part of the proceeds of the sale of debentures is sold while any part of the debentures remains outstanding, the net proceeds of the sale must be applied towards the amount of principal and interest then outstanding on the debentures. The treasurer of a board in respect of which a sum is required by law to be set aside for a sinking fund shall prepare and lay before the board every year before the board adopts the estimates a statement showing what amount will be required for that purpose.

Secondly, if the proceeds of the debentures are more than is required for the purposes for which the debentures were issued, the board must, if the debentures are redeemable and there is enough money, redeem debentures of the latest maturity. If that cannot be done, the excess money must be applied towards the annual payments of principal and interest on the debentures.

Thirdly, if all or any part from the sale or pledge of debentures is not required for the purposes for which the debentures were issued, it may be applied to buy back the debentures or to meet other capital expenditures of the board.

If, on the other hand, insufficient money is raised on the sale of all of debentures of a board and all or part of the amount of the deficit is required for the purposes for which the board issued the debentures, the board must make sure that:

(a) the amount required is added to the amount to be raised in the first year for the payment of principal and interest on the debentures and the amount to be set aside in the first year is increased accordingly; or

(b) the amount required is raised by the issuance of other debentures for the same or similar purposes.

Debt and Financial Obligation Limits[10]

A board cannot, without Ministry approval, exceed the prescribed limits for:

(a) long-term debt payable beyond the term for which the members of the board were elected; and

(b) long-term obligations, being other financial commitments, liabilities and contractual obligations payable beyond the term for which the members of the board were elected, including lease agreements.

The debt limit of a board is determined by subtracting from 10% of its estimated revenue fund expenditures for the year 62% of payments for the year for the long-term debt and other long-term obligations.

Before authorizing any specific work that would require the incurring of a long-term debt or financial obligation, the board must have its treasurer calculate updated limits using the most recent debt and financial obligations and liability limits information available. The updated debt limit is obtained by subtracting from the limit previously determined 62% of the estimated annual amount payable for the proposed project with which the board intends to proceed. The treasurer calculates 62% of the estimated annual amount payable by the board in respect of the proposed work and, if that amount exceeds the amount of the updated debt limit, the board must obtain the approval of the Minister before authorizing the work.

Short-Term Borrowing

A board can borrow, for any purpose for which the board has authority to spend money, any money in a fund established by the board that is not immediately required by the board for the purposes of the fund. This power does not extend to borrowing from a sinking fund, a retirement fund or money in an education development charges account under an education development charges by-law.

---

[10] See footnote 6, *supra*.

At the first meeting of a board after a regular election, the treasurer must report to the board on all borrowings under this power which have not been repaid.

Current Borrowing

A board can also by resolution authorize the treasurer and the chair or vice-chair to borrow from time to time money that the board considers necessary to meet current expenditures, including debt charges, of the board until the current revenue has been received. The total of these borrowings that have not been repaid and any accrued interest on them cannot exceed the unreceived balance of the estimated revenues of the board as set out in the estimates adopted for the fiscal year.

For this purpose, "estimated revenues" do not include revenues derivable or derived from the sale of assets, current borrowings, the issue of debentures or from a surplus, including arrears of taxes and proceeds from the sale of assets. "Current revenue", "estimated revenues" and "revenues" do not include revenue from education development charges.

The Minister can approve borrowings in excess of the amounts authorized by the Act by a board which is subject to an order made under Division D of Part IX of the Act, vesting control and charge over the administration of the affairs of the board in the Ministry.

INVESTMENTS[11]

The Act authorizes a board to invest in securities prescribed by regulation any money of the board in its general fund, capital fund or reserve fund which is not immediately needed by the board. A board can also advance money from its general fund or reserve funds that it does not immediately require to the board's capital fund as interim financing of board capital undertakings. These advances must be made repayable on or before the day on which the board requires the money and any interest or other earnings on the advance must be credited to the fund from which it was advanced.

Board Investments

Before a board invests in a security, it must, if it has not already done so, adopt a statement of the board's investment policies and goals. A board can only invest in the following securities, expressed and payable in Canadian dollars:

---

[11] See s. 241 of the Act and *Eligible Investments*, O. Reg. 471/97.

(a) bonds, debentures, promissory notes or other evidence of indebtedness issued or guaranteed by:

    (i)   Canada or a province or territory of Canada;

    (ii) an agency of Canada or a province or territory of Canada;

    (iii) a municipality in Canada;

    (iv) a board or similar entity in Canada; or

    (v) the Municipal Finance Authority of British Columbia.

(b) bonds, debentures, promissory notes or other evidence of indebtedness of a corporation if:

    1. The bond, debenture or other evidence of indebtedness is secured by the assignment to a trustee, as defined in the *Trustee Act*,[12] of payments that Canada or a province or territory has agreed to make or is required to make under a federal, provincial or territorial statute.

    2. The payments referred to para. 1 are sufficient to meet the amounts payable under the bond, debenture or other evidence of indebtedness, including the amounts payable at maturity.

(c) deposit receipts, deposit notes, certificates of deposit or investment, acceptances or similar instruments issued, guaranteed or endorsed by:

    (i) a bank listed in Schedule I of the *Bank Act*;[13]

    (ii) a loan corporation or trust corporation registered under the *Loan and Trust Corporations Act*;[14]

    (iii) a credit union or league to which the *Credit Unions and Caisses Populaires Act, 1994* applies; or

    (iv) the Province of Ontario Savings Office.

(d) bonds, debentures or evidence of long-term indebtedness issued or guaranteed by:

    (i) the Canadian Bond Rating Service Inc. as "AA-" or higher;

    (ii) the Dominion Bond Rating Service Ltd. as "AA(low)" or higher;

    (iii) Moody's Investors Services Inc. as "Aa3" or higher; or

    (iv) by Standard and Poor's Inc. as "AA-" or higher.

        If an investment falls below this standard, the board must sell the investment within 90 days after the day the investment falls below the standard.

(e) short-term securities, the terms of which provide that the principal and interest shall be fully repaid no later than three days after the day the investment was made, issued by:

---

[12] R.S.O. 1990, c. T.23 (as amended to 1994, c. 27).

[13] S.C. 1991, c. 46 (as amended to 1998, c. 36).

[14] R.S.O. 1990, c. L.25 (as amended to 1997, c. 28).

(i) the board of governors of a college of applied arts and technology established under s. 5 of the *Ministry of Colleges and Universities Act*;[15]

(ii) a degree granting institution as authorized under s. 3 of the *Degree Granting Act*;[16] or

(iii) a board as defined in the *Public Hospitals Act*.[17]

A board can continue to hold an investment expressed and payable in the currency of the United States of America or the United Kingdom which it held before January 1, 1998.

Investments of Old Boards

Where an old board or authority had made an investment before January 1, 1998, in bonds, debentures or other debt of a corporation, the new board may continue to hold them, if they are rated:

(a) by the Canadian Bond Rating Service Inc. as "AA-" or higher;

(b) by the Dominion Bond Rating Service Ltd. as "AA(low)" or higher;

(c) by Moody's Investors Services Inc. as "Aa3" or higher; or

(d) by Standard and Poor's Inc. as "AA-" or higher.

However, if the rating of the investment falls below the standard, the board must sell the investment within 90 days after the day the investment falls below the standard.

Treasurer's Reports

Every board which has an investment in a security must have the treasurer of the board prepare and provide to the board, each year or more frequently if required by the board, an investment report containing:

(a) a statement about the performance of the portfolio of investments of the board during the period covered by the report;

(b) a description of the estimated proportion of the total investments of a board that are invested in its own long-term and short-term securities to the total investment of the board with a description of the change, if any, in that estimated proportion since the previous year's report;

(c) the treasurer's opinion on whether or not all investments were made in accordance with the investment policies and goals adopted by the board;

---

[15] R.S.O. 1990, c. M.19 (as amended to 1993, c. 27, Sch.).

[16] R.S.O. 1990, c. D.5.

[17] R.S.O. 1990, c. P. 40 (as amended to 1997, c. 15).

(d) a record of the date of each transaction in or disposal of its own securities, including a statement of the purchase and sale price of each security; and

(e) any information that the board may require or that, in the opinion of the treasurer, should be included.

SUPERVISION OF BOARD'S FINANCIAL AFFAIRS

The Act under Division D of Part IX does not confer on the Minister general powers of supervision over boards' finances or a power to intervene in a board's affairs when the Minister thinks fit.[18] Rather, the purpose of Division D is to enable intervention by the Minister when a board is in financial difficulty.

The first step necessary to bring Division D into operation is the appointment by the Minister of an accountant or a Ministry employee to conduct an investigation. With one possible exception, the Minster's power to direct an investigation can be exercised only upon the happening of specific events, that is, if:

(a) the financial statements of the board for a fiscal year or the auditor's report on the statements indicate that the board had a deficit for that year;

(b) the board fails to pay any of its debentures or instruments or interest on them, after payment of the debenture, instrument or interest is due and has been demanded; or

(c) the board fails to pay any of its other debts or liabilities when due and default in payment is occasioned from financial difficulties affecting the board.

The possible exception is that the powers may also be exercised if the Minister "has concerns about the board's ability to meet the financial obligations".[19]

There is no subjective aspect to the first three events. The circumstances giving rise to the exercise of the powers must exist in fact and recourse could be had by a board to the courts for a determination of whether the necessary conditions exist.

There are adequately defined standards. Whether or not a board is in deficit or default is a readily assessable standard, a matter of accounting. The legislation imposes a requirement that boards not be in deficit. If a board is in deficit, it is not being governed "according to law".

---

[18] See Division D, "Supervision of Boards' Financial Affairs", ss. 257.30-257.52.
[19] Section 257.30(1)(d).

"Concerns", on the other hand, are subjective. What provokes anxiety in one mind may be of no worry to a mind of more optimistic caste. The courts are reluctant to accord deference to executive opinion or belief where there is no discernible rationale or factual basis therefor. The "concern" would have to be real and reasonable, not fanciful or arising by whim.

The issue is not solely one of textual interpretation of the legislation itself. Intervention by the province in the internal affairs of a board has to be measured against the protections afforded explicitly to separate schools by s. 93(1) of the Constitution.

The constitutional ramifications were canvassed extensively in the litigation which arose from the intervention in 1915 by the Minister of Education in the affairs of the Ottawa Separate School Board.[20] The education legislation in force at that time granted sweeping powers to the Minister where, in the opinion of the Minister, a board failed to comply with any of the provisions of the statute. The powers included Ministerial suspension of the rights, powers and privileges of a board and the appointment of a commission to exercise the powers of the board.

The very existence of these powers was held by the Privy Council to be an unconstitutional interference with s. 93(1) rights:

> The case before their Lordships is not that of a mere interference with a right or privilege, but of a provision which enables it to be withdrawn *in toto* for an indefinite time. Their Lordships have no doubt that the power so given would be exercised with wisdom and moderation, but it is the creation of the power and not its exercise that is subject to objection, and the objection would not be removed even though the powers conferred were never exercised at all. To give authority to withdraw a right or privilege under these conditions necessarily operates to the prejudice of the class of person affected by the withdrawal.[21]

Ontario amended the legislation and the constitutionality of the amendments was upheld.[22] The amendments limited both Ministerial powers and their exercise. An order placing a separate school board under supervision could be made only where the board was neglecting or refusing to carry out its responsibilities according to law. A supervision order was not indefinite; it was limited by the requirement that powers be restored when it appeared that the law will be complied with. Any question of whether the circumstances justified the appointment or continuance of a supervisory commission could be determined by a court.

---

[20] *Ottawa Separate School Trustees v. Ottawa (City)* (1916), 30 D.L.R. 770 (Ont. C.A.), revd 32 D.L.R. 10 (P.C.).

[21] *Supra*, at p. 13.

[22] *Ottawa Separate Schools (Re)* (1917), 40 D.L.R. 465 (Ont. C.A.).

Now under Division D of the Act and on the assumption that the Minister has good ground, the Minister can appoint an investigator to undertake an investigation and report in writing to the Minister with a copy to the secretary of the board. If the investigation discloses evidence of financial default or probable financial default, a deficit or a probable deficit, or serious financial mismanagement, and if the report recommends that control and charge over the administration of the affairs of the board should be vested in the Ministry, Cabinet may make an order vesting in the Ministry control and charge over the administration of the affairs of the board.

However, the Minister's power to intervene is not limited to circumstances in which an investigator has recommended that the Minister take charge and control of the board. The Minister reviews the report from the investigator and can give any directions to the board that the Minister considers advisable to address the financial affairs of the board. These Ministerial directions can be given whether or not the investigation has disclosed actual or probable deficit, default or mismanagement.

If the Minister advises Cabinet that he or she is of the opinion that the board has failed to comply with a direction, Cabinet can make an order to vest in the Ministry control and charge over the administration of the affairs of the board. If Cabinet makes such an order, the Minister has control and charge over the board generally with respect to any matter in any way affecting the board's affairs, including employees, estimates, accounting, audit, borrowing, assets, debt and money.

The Minister's powers include the power to:

(a) make any orders that he or she considers advisable to carry out the provisions of Division D or any agreement made under it;

(b) make rules governing anything done under Division D;

(c) bring injunction proceedings to prevent the exercise by a board of any of its powers not been approved by the Minister where approval is required under Division D;

(d) on the notice, if any, that the Minister considers appropriate, do or order done anything necessary to carry out a Ministerial order, direction or decision and may exercise all the powers of the board for the purpose, under its name; and

(e) dismiss from office any board officer or employee who fails to carry out any order, direction or decision of the Minister.

A board and each of its members, officers and employees is obliged to comply with the orders, directions and decisions of the Minister in any matter relating to the administration of the affairs of the board. The failure, knowingly, to comply with any such order, direction or decision is an offence. A member of the board who votes contrary to any such order, direction or decision is also guilty of an offence.

If a board applies any of its funds other than as ordered or authorized by the Minister, the members of the board who voted for the application are:

(a) jointly and severally liable for the amount and it can be recovered in a court of competent jurisdiction; and

(b) disqualified for five years from holding any office for which elections are held under the *Municipal Elections Act, 1996*[23] or the *Education Act.*

In view of the serious ramifications of disobedience of a direction from the Minister, it may be asked whether the courts have any role in cases of alleged misuse of the statutory powers. The expressed intent of the legislation is to answer that question in the negative.

The Act gives to the Minister "exclusive jurisdiction as to all matters arising under this Division or out of the exercise by the board or any person of any of the powers conferred by this Division, and that jurisdiction is not open to question or review in any proceeding or by any court".[24] The Act also gives to Cabinet exclusive jurisdiction as to the making of a vesting order and that jurisdiction is also not open to question or review in any proceeding or by any court.

Some of these issues were canvassed by Cumming J. in the *Bill 160 Case.*[25] With regard to the privative clause, he doubted its effectiveness and questioned the ability of the legislation to preclude court scrutiny, noting that the privative clause could not exclude a determination of whether a s. 93(1) violation had occurred in a given trusteeship and, in fact, if such was the intent of the legislation it would be invalid as it is not within the constitutional powers and authority of the legislature to do so. Left for future determination was the extent to which the court could intervene on other grounds.

Cumming J. upheld the constitutional validity of Division D but there are questionable aspects to his reasoning. He stated:

> The precondition for the imposition of a vesting order is a deficit or default, or likelihood thereof. It appears that, given the Minister's power to make directions, a deficit or default may not be an absolute precondition, but I am unconcerned by that ambiguity, because the condition for lifting a vesting order is absolute and not subject to discretion. The order *has* to be lifted if it is clear that there is no deficit or default.[26]

---

[23] S.O. 1996, c. 32, s. 1(1), Sch. (as amended to 1997, c. 31).

[24] *Education Act*, s. 257.40(1).

[25] (1998), 162 D.L.R. (4th) 257 (Ont. Ct. (Gen. Div.)), appeal allowed in part 172 D.L.R. (4th) 193 (C.A.).

[26] *Supra*, at p. 302 (Gen. Div.).

He goes on to find that the section which allows a vesting order:

> . . . where the Minister makes a direction regarding a board's financial affairs and, in the opinion of the Minister, the direction is not followed . . . is flawed, but not fatally so . . . the direction must still be, with regard to financial affairs, an important modification . . . [and] although there is discretion there, there is absolutely none as to when the trusteeship *must* be lifted, i.e. if the financial records disclose that there is in actuality no deficit.[27]

The section which the judge relied on for this conclusion[28] provides that:

1. Cabinet shall revoke a vesting order if Cabinet is of the opinion that the affairs of a board no longer need to be administered under Division D.
2. Cabinet shall revoke an order if the financial statements of a board for a fiscal year and the auditor's report on the statements submitted to the Ministry indicate that the board did not have a deficit for the fiscal year.

The first of these powers is dependent upon the (probably unreviewable) opinion of the Cabinet. The second is limited to the board not having a deficit. But the vesting order may have had nothing to do with a deficit. It could have arisen from a failure to meet or difficulty in meeting financial obligations. The lifting of vesting orders arising out of non-deficit circumstances is presumably left to Cabinet opinion.

---

[27] *Supra*, at pp. 304-305.
[28] *Education Act*, s. 257.50.

Index